They Call Me Agnes

Agnes

They Call Me Agnes

A Crow Narrative
Based on the Life
of Agnes Yellowtail Deernose

By Fred W. Voget
Assisted by Mary K. Mee

University of Oklahoma Press : Norman and London

By Fred W. Voget

Osage Indians: Osage Research Report I (New York and London, 1974)
A History of Ethnology (New York, 1975)
Storia dell'etnologia contemporanea (Roma-Bari, Italy, 1984)
The Shoshoni-Crow Sun Dance (Norman, 1984)
They Call Me Agnes: A Crow Narrative Based on the Life of Agnes Yellowtail Deernose (Norman, 1995)

This book is published with the generous assistance of The McCasland Foundation, Duncan, Oklahoma.

Library of Congress Cataloging-in-Publication Data

Voget, Fred W.
    They call me Agnes : a Crow narrative based on the life of Agnes Yellowtail Deernose / by Fred W. Voget ; assisted by Mary K. Mee.
        p.   cm.
    Includes bibliographical references and index.
    ISBN: 0–8061–2695–7 (alk. paper)
    1. Deernose, Agnes Yellowtail.   2. Crow Indians—Biography.
3. Crow Indians—Social life and customs.   I. Mee, Mary K.
II. Title.
E99.C92D448   1995
973'.04975'0092—dc20   94–38872
    [B]   CIP

The paper in this book meets the guidelines for permanence and durability of the Committee on Production Guidelines for Book Longevity of the Council on Library Resources, Inc. ∞

1   2   3   4   5   6   7   8   9   10

This book is dedicated to
Donnie and Agnes Deernose
and to all Crow
who have struggled
to find a path to the future
with personal meaning,
despite the challenges,
ambiguities, and conflicts that
the confrontation between
traditional Crow culture
and American culture
brought into their lives.

Contents

Illustrations

Photographs

Maps

Preface

This narrative is about life on the Crow Indian Reservation from around 1910 to the present and is based on the personal experiences of Donnie and Agnes Deernose. Agnes became the principal narrator after Donnie's untimely death. The narrative reveals some of the hardships faced within the reservation system as the Crow struggled to overcome the restrictive weight of limited resources and tried to achieve a secure, independent, and personally satisfying economic existence.

Both Donnie and Agnes reflect the profound influence of their fathers, who warned them what the future held for Crow youth without educational skills in a world increasingly ruled by Yellow Eyes, as the Crow called the invading Americans. Their fathers recognized that the old life as they had known it was over. Indians were increasingly called upon to make judgmental decisions on a wide range of changes being forced upon them through administrative rules and processes under the control of the agent. At the time men may have been more sensitive to what lay ahead than were women, since men were more directly involved in the political changes whereas the women were better able to maintain the traditional continuity of their lives through domestic and childbearing roles.

In the course of his life Donnie followed the traditional role of men as spiritual leaders, protectors, and providers for their families. He did so through an active participation and leadership in the Baptist mission church and by learning new skills, working hard, and setting a course that would lead to efficient management of cattle ranching. He also dedicated himself to the welfare of his people by actively participating in political and economic affairs.

Agnes followed the traditional role expectations for women while making the Baptist church a dominant force and guide for her life. Men traditionally were heads of the families, and she accorded that place to Donnie without question. However, when Crow law in some cases gave her certain rights and privileges, she did not hesitate to make her own decisions.

The lives of both Donnie and Agnes emphasize the continuing importance of religion in sustaining traditional Crow values and customs of the reservation culture and in helping to adjust during the forcible transition to the values and rules of American society and culture.

In a work of this kind one is always assisted in ways great and small by many. Some of those who helped me have passed away. Donnie and Agnes made the work possible by sharing a portion of their lives and experiences. For special information I am indebted to Yellow Woman, Amy Whiteman, Bobby Bends, Bill and Ferale Pease, and Frederick V. Lefthand, and to Joe Turnsback Plenty and Pete Lefthand for their interpretations between 1939 and 1946. I owe special thanks to Joe Medicine Crow for providing the background of ceremonies that the Crow invented or borrowed during the later development of the Crow reservation culture, and also for the French line of descent in the Yellowtail genealogy. I am grateful to the American Philosophical Society for the grant that made the start of this research possible. Special thanks is due also to Dr. George Spindler for helpful assistance.

Agnes has furnished family photographs, and I am especially grateful to Mr. Dennis Sanders of the Hardin Photo Service for making available photographs of the Yellowtail family from his collection of Crow Indian photographs. Photographs of Agnes and Kay, Donnie and Agnes's home, and the Baptist mission church were taken by the author.

For details of historic Crow culture, I am reminded of the debt to those who recorded and interpreted Crow life during their buffalo-hunting days, notably, Robert H. Lowie, Edward S. Curtis, William Wildschut (manuscripts edited by John C. Ewers and Peter Nabokov), fur traders Edwin Denig and François Larocque, and Frank B. Linderman, biographer of Chief Plenty Coups and of Pretty Shield.

In the description of Crow culture, I have concentrated on the origins and nature of the sacred and on how the Crow organized their society for the management of sacred power to ease and control life's hardships and challenges. Where ethnographic description has not supplied a background to action, I have introduced inferential interpretations to convey an understanding of the contexts and apparent intentions of Crow ceremonialists.

To ease the pronunciation of Crow words introduced into the text, I have followed common English phonetic transcription. For example, *maxpe* becomes *makpay*.

The Crow tribal name has been rendered in a multitude of ways, ranging from Absaraka, Absarakee, Absaroka, and Apsaruke to Apsaloka and Apsaalooke. Crow Indians themselves give different phonetic transcriptions. Transcriptions of the Crow Bilingual Program emphasize current trends in which "l" phonetically is taking precedence over the traditional "r." I have followed the sound pattern prevailing before World War II, which is commonly found in ethnographic reports. The Crow commemorated the Treaty of 1868 with a centennial publication entitled *Absaraka*.

Dr. Barbara Loeb, Professor Euna Rose He-Does-It, and Mardell Plainfeather read the manuscript, and I wish to thank them for their helpful criticisms and suggestions. My thanks also to Mr. Tim Bernardis, Librarian, Little Big Horn College, for his special assistance. My grateful thanks also is due to Sally Bennett, who edited the manuscript, and to Mildred Logan, associate editor, and the staff of the University of Oklahoma Press for preparing the manuscript for publication.

My thanks to my wife, Kay, for her helpful editorial assistance, and to Fred Hyde and Jane Voget for their good suggestions with regard to the Introduction. I also wish to thank John and Julie van Woye and Dennis and Geri Sanders for their help in making this book possible.

FRED W. VOGET

Portland, Oregon

Introduction

When I was a graduate student at Yale University in 1938, the Anthropology Department was engaged in a cross-cultural survey that included approximately 275 world societies. One of the groups selected for this research was the Crow Indian tribe of Montana, who were considered to be a typical hunting society in a Plains environment. The intent was to assemble a world sample that would provide more exact comparisons, which then would reveal conditions and processes governing a wide range of customs regulating human behavior.

The Crow had been well researched by Robert Lowie, and my task was to fill out materials that had not been covered in sufficient depth or had not been touched upon in the historic and ethnographic accounts. In preparation I read the available literature and extracted materials under standardized categories developed in an outline of cultural materials. And so, on a late summer day in 1939 I drove my Model A Ford into Lodge Grass, Montana, on the Crow Reservation.

My first sight of the reservation was a verdant valley crossed by the Big Horn and Little Big Horn rivers leisurely winding their way side by side until they came together at Hardin. Sunlit clouds cast their shadows on the land below, and the great expanse of sky stretched as

far as the eye could see to the shining Big Horn Mountains. I came to love the land and to respect and admire
the Crow people. What started out as an interesting
research project turned out to be an important part of
my life's work. Some of these people became not only my
informants and interpreters but also my treasured and
lifelong friends. I was to return to this special place
many times throughout the years.

The Crow historically were buffalo hunters of the
Northern Plains. During the 1600s they had broken
away from village-dwelling Hidatsa located along the
Missouri River in North Dakota and had worked their
way west into the area of the Yellowstone River and the
Big Horn Mountains (Clark 1982:195; Curtis 1970:38–39;
Lowie 1918:272–75; Voget 1990; Wood and Downer
1977). Although continuing to raise sacred tobacco, the
Crow abandoned the cultivation of corn, beans, and
squash and pursued the life of hunters. They feasted on
buffalo and elk; clothed themselves in tailored skin
shirts, leggings, moccasins, and dresses; and housed
themselves in buffalo-hide tipis. With the coming of the
horse early in the 1700s, they became important middlemen in the trade between western Indians and the
Hidatsa and Mandan villagers of North Dakota. Crow
brought horses, leather goods, compound bows, buffalo
robes, and shells from the West Coast and Plateau Indians in exchange for European goods, knives, cloth,
beads, and local corn (Ewers 1968; Taylor 1981; Voget
1984;4–12; Wood 1980).

The Crow developed a reputation as canny traders,
skilled horse raiders, and courageous fighters. By
Northern Plains standards they were wealthy and the
envy of their neighbors. No tribe could equal the colorful grandeur of a Crow parade when they approached a

village or post for trade. Early traders, explorers, and artists were impressed with their tall and athletic build and their proud and stately appearance as they displayed the ornamental beauty of the skin clothing and buffalo robes that their women produced with painstaking skill (Catlin 1973:1:46–47; Denig 1985:154–55; Maximilian 1966:346). To early French explorers the Crow were *les beaux hommes*, or Handsome Men (La Vérendrye 1927). Later French traders called them *gens du corbeau(x)*, or the People of the Crow. Perhaps traders were struck by the blackbird mounted on the heads of leaders of horse raids who trusted the blackbird's medicine to lead them unerringly to enemy horses (Nabokov 1970: 152). The Crow called themselves Absaroka or Absorokee and identified themselves with motions of a bird flying (Kurz 1937:252). No one has been able to identify with certainty the big-beaked bird to which their name, Absarokee, refers, although Plenty Coups considered the name to mean Children of the Raven (Linderman 1962:51–52). Another possibility is the eagle, which the Crow called Big Bird, especially when the eagle (in his role of Thunderbird) hurled thunderbolts of sacred power.

In later decades of their buffalo-hunting existence, the Crow increasingly were forced to defend their homeland from the intrusions of the more numerous Blackfeet, Sioux, Arapaho, and Cheyenne. The pressures of tribal enemies who coveted their favorable trade location and the abundance of their game led the Crow to ally themselves with the forces of the United States and to furnish scouts for General George Armstrong Custer (Voget 1984:14–15; Weist 1977).

The Crow moved to their present reservation situated between Billings, Montana, and Sheridan, Wyoming, in

1883–1884. They surrendered some 30 million acres for a guaranteed reserve of 8 million acres, but further land cessions eventually reduced the reservation to less than 3 million acres. Their population also suffered a sharp decline because of the unsanitary life, malnutrition, and diseases to which they were exposed on the reservation. The shock of passing from a life in which they were their own masters to one of complete dependence on handouts of food, clothing, and housing brought grave dislocations in personal and family living. Life as they had known it had come to a standstill, and their lives were suspended in limbo. They faced changes that would alter their entire way of life. Missionaries, priests, educators, storekeepers, and settlers were unsympathetic and joined the Crow Indian agent in urging and coercing them to give up their "superstitious" and "immoral" ways.

During these difficult and humiliating years, the Crow drew upon the only resource with which they were familiar and could manage—namely, their traditional ways. More so than other Plains tribes, the Crow succeeded in developing a reservation culture that preserved core beliefs, values, social relations, and mutual obligations of their culture while conforming to the formal demands of dress, schooling, church, and legalisms of the local American culture (Voget 1984:16–28; Voget 1987).

During the 1930s, Crow life had changed little from early reservation times. Old men still wore the high-crowned black reservation hats, and some still wore their hair in two braids, a fashion borrowed from Nez Percé Indians during the 1870s. Some also had a short medicine braid hanging down the back of the head. However, young men had no braids. In conformance with the rules of the government boarding schools they were forced to attend, their braids had been cut off. Older women wore two braids and painted a red streak down the middle part, and both men and women tied the ends of the braids with small strips of red, blue, or green cloth or ribbon. Outdoors, women wore head scarves of dark cotton and draped a woolen blanket, usually a Pendleton, around their shoulders very much as their grandmothers had done with their buffalo robes. Women customarily wore loose-fitting cotton print dresses that they had made themselves, cinched in the middle by a broad leather or beaded belt with an ammunition-type pouch attached for carrying silver dollars and change. Their yellow or white high-top moccasins almost reached the knee, and on rainy or snowy days they slipped black rubbers over the moccasins. Older women continued the tanning and beading skills that had made the Crow famous. Men worked with horses and cattle and periodically hunted deer and elk, but they found it difficult to maintain the traditional image of men as providers for their families.

The Crow were still able to live some of their traditional life. Medicine bundles were hidden away and brought out in spring and fall for family veneration. Some had taken over the Peyote religion as part of their Indian identity and used traditional healing for those who were afraid to go to the hospital. A number of enterprising men gathered together a few related families, and at rodeos and fairs in Sheridan, Billings, and Cheyenne, they dramatized some of the old life in dance, song, and horse racing.

Despite forces operating to alter their culture, the Crow during the 1930s were quite isolated from the mainstream of American life in a physical sense as well as in social and psychological ways. This was true even though a paved state highway ran through the towns of Crow Agency, Lodge Grass, and Wyola and some were learning to drive automobiles.

Lodge Grass and Crow Agency were the only towns on the reservation with clustered populations and a recognizable commercial development. Although Lodge Grass had a greater economic development than other district settlements, it lacked the agency with its administrators and supporting staff, as well as a hospital, which were located at Crow Agency. Lodge Grass had a population of about eight hundred, of which nearly 50 percent were Indians. Several hundred Crow lived in ghettolike clapboard houses of two or three rooms, some with patched or broken-out windows. Various Indian families were scattered throughout the town, and nearby, families had built a small log cabin camp known as Eshebea, or Muddy Mouth. Lodge Grass contained three grocery stores, an auto supply store, a garage, two service stations, a post office, a drugstore, two hotels of sorts, a bowling alley, a poolroom, two barber shops, a movie house, and two or three cafés. Non-Indian pawnbrokers traded cash for dance outfits or heirloom objects. A bootlegger operated in discreet obscurity in a small house across the Little Big Horn River, well camouflaged with bushes. Crow gathered almost weekly at the octagonal Eshebea hall for social dances, giveaways, and box socials. Lodge Grass mirrored the social and psychological distance separating Indians and non-Indians, who fraternized little on or off the reservation. Restaurants in Sheridan, Hardin, and Billings posted signs stating, "We reserve the right to refuse service," and "No Indians or dogs allowed." (In 1947 my wife and I had a firsthand experience with this bias when we were evicted from the Lodge Grass Hotel because Indians tried to visit me there.)

A grade school and high school stood on the bluff above Lodge Grass. The Crow adopted basketball as their preeminent sport after their long-braided players in 1919 brought home a regional championship. The region extended south to Denver and Salt Lake, north to the Canadian border, and east to Devils Lake, North Dakota. The team was called the Lodge Grass Farmers because at the time the Crow were trying hard to become farmers. The players wore their hair in a Crow-style pompadour in front, and when playing they tied their three braids at the back. Five of the six-man team stood well over six feet tall, and among the Crow this earned them the nickname of "Telephone Poles." Basketball was not yet fully organized by districts then, and the team played and defeated its challengers without using substitutes. All the players were in their early twenties. The team included Pete Lefthand (6'2"), Mortimer Plentyhawk (6'7"), John White Man Runs Him (6'7"), Art Bravo (5'11"), Reuben Spotted Horse (6'4"), and Hartford Black Eagle (6'2").

When I arrived I noticed that Crow boys constantly practiced at shooting baskets through barrel hoops raised on poles at Eshebea and elsewhere. Two years before, the town had been split because some residents alleged that Indian players were favored over Whites in the high school basketball team. Non-Indian parents were up in arms because they claimed their sons had little chance to make the team.

Two churches served the Lodge Grass Christian community. The Crow Indian Baptist mission was established in 1903, and St. Ann's Catholic Church in 1904. However, churches failed to unite Indians and non-

Indians in a common brotherhood, and it was customary in an integrated church for each to sit on opposite sides of the church.

In 1887 Congress passed the Allotment Act, which was designed to provide Indians with an individual land base to expedite their becoming citizens. Lands not allotted at the time the reservation was established were to be reserved for future descendants. In 1903 the Supreme Court determined that Congress was empowered to open reservation lands to settlement, provided it was in the public interest, regardless of any treaties (Prucha 1990:201–203). In the 1903 decision, the Supreme Court asserted that the power granted to Congress to make treaties also allowed Congress to break treaties inasmuch as congressional power was political and not subject to court challenge. Subsequently, Senator Thomas Walsh of Montana introduced a bill to open the so-called surplus lands of the Crow Reservation to homestead settlement. The Crow realized that opening their reservation to White settlers would jeopardize their hopes to manage their own lands and resources and would threaten the future of their children. In April of 1917 Robert Yellowtail, Agnes's oldest brother, accompanied the delegation of warrior-chiefs, headed by Chief Plenty Coups, to Washington. The delegation was to meet with the Senate Indian Affairs committee for the final hearing before the bill went to the Senate, and the Crow went to the capital to oppose the bill. Robert Yellowtail was 27 years old, well educated, and articulate. The Crow chose him as their spokesman.

In preparation for this new kind of warfare, Plenty Coups and the warrior-chiefs took their wartime medicine bundles to overcome the power of the senators. They collected buffalo chips from the Washington zoo, and in a ceremony in their room they burned the chips with a mixture of sweetgrass and Nez Percé root incenses. As each warrior stirred his incense and sent smoke heavenward to the Creator, he sang his medicine song.

The warriors' ceremony prepared the way for victory. Robert Yellowtail captivated the senators with his brilliant and passionate arguments, and for four and one-half hours he "turned the Senate hearing into one of silent reflection" (Harcey and Croone 1993:177). When Yellowtail had finished, Senator Robert La Follette of Wisconsin stood and led the response in support of the Crow. Senator Walsh withdrew his bill, and the challenge of White homesteading of the Crow Reservation was laid to rest.

However, the allotment of arable acreage that was worked out in the compromise left no reservation land for distribution to Crow born after 1921. The population of the Crow in 1920 was still in decline and numbered less than two thousand. To meet the conditions of the allotment of 1,040 acre-units per person, the Crow were forced to adopt and enroll Blackfeet, Cree, and other tribesmen married to Crow on the reservation. Some non-Indians residing on the reservation also were allotted lands. Except for the vagaries of inheritance, the subsequent landless generations created were deprived of the modest but relatively stable income others enjoyed through land rentals. Rentals were usually arranged by agency officials without full consultation with the Indian owners.

In the 1930s changes were under way that would help instil a fresh confidence in Crow ways. The new commissioner of Indian affairs, John Collier, launched a plan of national recovery for Indians in 1934 that encouraged

Indians to make use of tribal values and religion to revitalize and integrate their communities (Prucha 1990:222–28). His program included economic development of reservation resources with more management in the hands of Indians. Robert Yellowtail was appointed superintendent of the Crow Indian Reservation.

When I first came to know Donnie and Agnes Deernose in 1939, they had been married for eight years and were staunch members of the Lodge Grass Baptist church. They were a friendly, personable, and handsome couple in their early thirties. Each had experienced an unhappy first marriage that had been arranged for each of them according to custom.

Donnie and Agnes were born and grew up at a time when the reservation culture was vibrant and drew people together in a year-round calendar of events patterned largely after American holidays. In Crow belief, dream-blessings bestowed by clan uncles and aunts were responsible for personal health and success. The recipient's clan relatives feasted these uncles and aunts at giveaways and sent them home with blankets, scarves, dress goods, and money in repayment. On weekends, the Crow socialized at the local district dance hall, and in the winter they gave training and instructions to the candidates who would be adopted into the Tobacco Society in the spring.

Donnie had already emerged as a prominent representative of Indian converts to the Baptist mission church. He also had served as a delegate to Baptist conventions and often spoke to church and business organizations off the reservation. As individuals, the Crow lived in the midst of two cultures, each of which exerted conflicting demands upon them. Because of their strong commitment to Christianity, Donnie and

Agnes seemingly had determined to follow American ways. Yet I knew that Donnie at the same time adhered to many Crow customs. For example, he strictly observed the Crow custom that forbade a son-in-law to speak directly to his mother-in-law or face her across the table, even though his mother-in-law lived with him and Agnes for nearly thirty-seven years.

Both Donnie and Agnes were good examples of how people adapted to change while retaining much of their old ways. Their personal narratives provide insights as to how individuals moved back and forth between two cultures and combined them in form as well as in psychological ways.

Our friendship grew during the years I was working on my thesis and teaching grades six to eight in the Lodge Grass Elementary School. Two of my students were Ataloa and Ferale Hogan, who had been adopted by Agnes and her mother. Agnes's only son, Bobby, was a star basketball player at the high school.

The war separated us, but we kept in touch and I returned later for two- to three-week visits. On one of these visits in 1956, when I drove up to their house, Agnes came out and greeted us. "Come in," she invited; "We want to tell you about our trip to Europe." Another time, in 1968, I sat with Agnes and Donnie and some of their relatives watching on television the funeral of Robert Kennedy, who had once visited the Crow Reservation. Everyone was silent and saddened, and Bobby asked, "Who will speak for us now?" On another visit in 1985, Agnes, Kay, and I had lunch together at the Lodge Grass Hotel. The hotel no longer publicized the "no Indians allowed" policy, and staff members treated us courteously.

Any personal narrative in its presentation and organization is shaped by the dialogue between the narrator and the interviewer. When we began, I asked Donnie and Agnes to tell of their life experiences as if they were recounting the events to their own people, to accent what was meaningful to them and to the Crow. They were both fluent in English, and during our conversations we agreed to begin with birth and family background and then move on to home life, schooling, church, marriage, and other important experiences in their lives. As they paused periodically in their narratives, I followed the Crow way and from time to time interjected an "Eh" sound and nodded to indicate my attention and interest and that I wanted them to continue. At times I requested additional details, and at the beginning of each new day I began with questions prompted by materials transcribed the night before.

Within a year after we started on the personal narratives, Donnie passed away from severe complications following a collision of his car with a truck. I attended Donnie's funeral and saw the great outpouring of grief and respect of the Crow for one of their most beloved leaders. As I was leaving for home, Agnes gave me Donnie's ring and cuff links and a medicine of Donnie's father's, which had thirteen pony beads representing, in all probability, the thirteen Crow clans.

Agnes and I continued with interviews that stretched over several summers during my two- and three-week visits to the Crow. My interviews with Agnes, as with Donnie, were taken down in a shorthand-notehand and took place at the kitchen table or in the yard under shade trees, usually near a clothesline to which strips of meat had been pinned to dry.

Personal narratives are vibrant, but incomplete, introductions to the lifeways of a people. There were some historical events and ceremonies, the details of which Donnie and Agnes did not know or could not completely remember. In these instances I interwove these background details with the narrative to maintain continuity and readability, as well as to bring out the cultural meaning of social situations and to give a rounded picture of what life on the reservation was like when they were growing up. Ethnographic descriptions supplied a few of the details, but most were contributed by various informants and from my own extensive notes taken when I was present at these special events. At times I rearranged narrative notes to fit in sequence. At times Agnes was her own editor. She talked freely about Donnie's death and funeral, but when Bobby died she never told me anything about it. I learned from others of his passing.

After Donnie died, Agnes was the principal narrator. To maintain an easy flow throughout her story, I expressed the material added in her own style as much as possible. These additional materials, probably ten percent, I introduced into the chapters as follows:

Chapter 2. "I'm Born a Crow Indian." This is mostly in Agnes's words, with supplemental information told me in 1939 by Yellow Woman of Pryor with regard to sleeping arrangements of pregnant women, puppies to induce the flow of milk, tobacco as a remedy for colic, ear piercing, and examples in the bestowal of names and the use of medicine necklaces for children.
Chapter 3. "My Family and Relations." The principal voice is Agnes's. Her son, Bobby, provided some information about the Yellowtail Dam, while Frederick Lefthand contributed notes on basketball and the procedure for use of the river to get rid of evil. Reflec-

tions on fathers and mothers are a composite of my own field notes and remarks by Agnes. Information about black as a symbol of victory and about men's and women's property was drawn from ethnographic sources (Curtis, Denig, Lowie) and from my own field notes.

Chapter 4. "Growing Up." This is Agnes's narrative, except for minor editing to bring out the Crow view of the mother's brother as an older brother and details regarding brother-sister respect taken from my field notes and ethnographic sources. Details of Old Man Coyote and his mother-in-law were drawn from Lowie's "Myths and Traditions of the Crow Indians." I used my own field notes regarding bestowal of an honor name during a political meeting and Crow emphasis on readiness when introducing skills to children.

Chapter 5. "School, Education, and Church." Agnes's is the principal voice. I drew on field notes to supplement Agnes's remarks and on Donnie's description of their activities during the war and his views on selling land and on education. I also utilized Lowie's description of the adoption procedure to fill in some details of Agnes's adoption as a Tobacco Society member.

Chapter 6. "Courtship and Marriage." Agnes is the principal narrator, except for passages dealing with American Indian Days, politics and the Yellowtail Dam, and Donnie's term as secretary of the tribal council, which are a composite of remarks by both Agnes and Donnie.

Chapter 7. "Life Without Donnie, The Complete Bear." This is Agnes's voice, except for my own notes added to the description of the funeral and giveaway only. The description of mourning in the old way and fear of the dead combines ethnographic data (Lowie and Leforge, edited by Marquis) and my own notes.

Chapter 8. "Celebrating the Year Together." This is a composite of many voices interwoven to bring out the nature and importance of these festive occasions. I used ethnographic description to emphasize the importance of the seasonal rhythm and of the sun's circuit for the present festive calendar, which begins in late summer in imitation of the good times celebrated in the fall during the Crow's buffalo days. Agnes remained a principal contributor with descriptions of their giveaway when Donnie was treasurer of the Crow Fair, Soldier Boys' Day, Thanksgiving, Christmas, Easter, Fourth of July, the preparation of festive foods, Amy's adoption as a whipper, praise songs, feasting clan uncles and aunts, Sunday Games, and summer camps.

Joe Medicine Crow contributed notes on the history of the Push and Long House dances, and I used the account of fur trader Denig to fill out background details on the Atsina woman made captive by the Crow around 1816, who inspired the dance known as Woman Chief. Activities of contemporary Night Hawk and Ree (Big Ear Hole) clubs at the New Year's Dance are based on information from Frederick V. Lefthand. Descriptions of the arrow throw at Pryor following the war and of the Sun Dance are from my own field notes and publications. Crow burial practices and fear of ghosts described under Memorial Day were derived from various sources (Curtis, Leforge, Lowie) and my own notes.

In May 1993, I went over the manuscript with Agnes to make sure that we were in agreement on details, and she was pleased with the way her narrative had been fitted

Agnes and Kay, 1986

into the contexts and changes of Crow reservation culture. Agnes's adopted daughter, Ferale, and her husband, Bill Pease, assisted with explanations and correc-
tions of dates and relationships where needed during
the reading of the manuscript. Agnes also took an active
part in the reading of the manuscript. We sat around
Ferale's big kitchen table with cups of coffee and doughnuts and spent three days reading, discussing, and
checking details. At one point in the reading of the part
about Donnie's death, Agnes sat with her eyes cast down
and her head lowered. I asked if we should stop for a
while and continue the next day, but she quickly replied,
"No, don't stop. Keep on reading." When we were finished, they all said they were sorry it ended.

When I saw Agnes in 1990, her home was still the
gathering place for friends, relatives, and grandchildren. Agnes loved to be with people and to be on the
go. She kept busy at the senior citizens' center and
worked at the Lodge Grass Town Hall as a general
maintenance person until 1992. When I saw her again in
May of 1993, Agnes still had her family home but was
spending much of her time with Ferale and Bill. She still
liked to be on the go and was busy working on a pair of
beaded moccasins she planned to wear to a powwow
that was scheduled the following weekend. She had
finished altering a pair of tiny moccasins that Ferale's
two-year-old granddaughter had outgrown by fitting a
piece of matching buckskin to extend the heel.

When we were ready to leave, they all said, "Come
again." Ferale reminded us that Crows do not like to say
goodbye but prefer at parting to say, "*Kadachee deawagaawek,*" which means, "I'll see you again."

Then Agnes accompanied us out into the yard and
stood beside the lilac hedge and waved until the car was

out of sight. At eighty-five, Agnes was still a striking woman with great dignity. She was dressed in the traditional style of her generation in a long-sleeved flowered dress that she had made. The dress was cinched at the waist by a wide leather belt with turquoise inlay, and she was wearing a necklace of blue beads and a silver bracelet with turquoise. She wore her hair, now white, parted in the middle with two braids. Earlier when we went out for lunch to the Purple Cow in Hardin, she added a fringed shawl and a dark blue head scarf. Ferale told us later that after we had gone, Agnes sat alone outside at the picnic table for almost two hours. When she came in, she told Ferale that she had "almost cried." Crows do not like to say goodbye.

Kadachee deawagaawek.

They Call Me Agnes

CHAPTER 1

Historic Crow and Reservation Culture

Historic Crow Culture

The reservation culture under which Agnes and Donnie grew up preserved the basic values, clan organization, and social reciprocities of Crow culture and society while accommodating to the formal, social, educational, and legal requirements of American culture. Crow simply poured the new wine of American culture into their own bottles by borrowing or substituting American elements while retaining the basic structure and procedures of their own culture (Voget 1980; Voget 1984:16–28; Voget 1987.

Historic Crow culture was largely the product of the horse and of the fur trade during the 1700s. During this time the Crow enjoyed the best of times as they took advantage of new economic opportunities and transformed themselves from pedestrian to mounted hunters, horse raiders, and intertribal middlemen. Introduction of the horse and of trade added quality and style to Crow life, including improvements in the size of tipis, ease of transportation, and the amount of available food and hides for robes and clothing. New opportunities for economic gain intensified competition for wealth and social reputations, which were based on military achievements and the distribution of wealth, especially

3

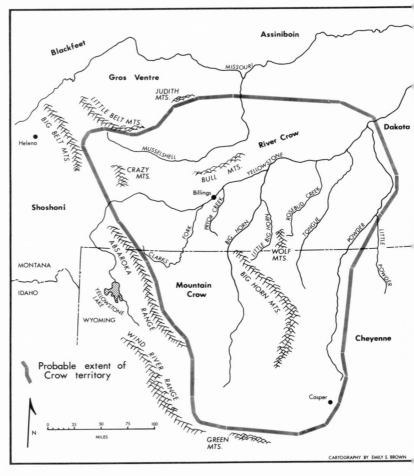

Map 1. Historic Crow Homeland

in horses. Horse raiding and revenge warfare milita-
rized Crow culture, and the warrior emerged as the ideal
personality type. Men achieved reputation, political influence, and leadership through standardized military
kudos in combination with dream prophecies bestowed
by spirit patrons. With the horse, Crow traveled faster
and farther than in the days when they trudged from
one camp to the next, using dogs to drag the small poles
for their hutlike tipis and to carry some of the burden-
some gear. The horse gave greater control over the hunt,
for they could drive numerous herdlets together and
slaughter hundreds of buffalo instead of dozens. They
could congregate in bands numbering from two to four
thousand instead of the two or three hundred during
their pedestrian days. The band united members from
the different matrilineal clans under a chief and became
the primary political unit attached to a regional territory
(Curtis 1970:8–20; Lowie 1935:3–17; Taylor 1981; Voget
1984:29–76; Voget 1990).

Spiritual Essence of the Universe

A belief that spiritual beings determined the outcome of
human events tempered the pragmatic approach of Crow
to life situations. Hence, they regulated their lives by
instructions and gifts of mystic power bestowed by
spiritual beings who had organized the world and governed its day-to-day operations by answering human
cries for help. For both private and public good, the
Crow depended on spiritual benefactors to find buffalo,
raid for horses, defeat enemies, control weather, cure
sickness, lead and safeguard camp movements, and
conduct ceremonies. In reality, the creation time never
had come to an end; throughout their history, individual

Crow in visions and in dream visitations continued to receive gifts of sacred power that they used in times of need for their own private benefit and for the benefit of the Crow people as a whole.

An original creator set the stars in their heavenly places and created the earth and all within it. He was known as First Maker, Starter or Maker Of All Things, The One Above, The Old White Man Above, The Above Person With Yellow Eyes, He That Hears Always, and He That Sees All Things (Clark 1982:136–38; Curtis 1970:52; Lowie 1935:231–32; Wildschut 1975:1–2). First Maker had so made the universe that stars, stones, insects, animals, birds, and even men and women could take on the form and behavior of spirits. Spirits were endowed with a special sacred energy or power, *makpay,* characteristic of their original animal natures and capabilities. They could appear interchangeably in their human or in their material earthly forms. Spirit persons with such "medicine" were known as Those That Have No Bodies, and their earthly counterparts were the Without Fires People, who appeared as buffalo, otters, hawks, eagles, rattlesnakes, and the myriad forms of animal life as well as rocks, trees, and plants. As eagle and buffalo revealed, some spirit persons were more powerful than others (Curtis 1970:52–54; Frey 1987:88ff.; Lowie 1918: 315–43).

Makpay, the omnipresent sacred essence, manifested itself in the white vapors of clouds and in the foggy mists rising from frosty earth, clothing the earth with a white blanket and at times turning trees that bordered streams into shadowy figures. First Maker was the embodiment of this vaporous essence, for he was not only The One Above but also The Old White Man Above.

The vaporous essence, *makpay,* in association with

soul, *erakay*, constituted the very core of being. Time and again, as Crow fasted high in the mountains, spirit persons approached them through cloud mists, and during ceremonies eagles and bears sometimes appeared in clouds. When set afire, tobacco changed into its soul-power form, drifting upward as a smoke-prayer to a watchful spirit person. Breath vapors rising heavenward on a frosty morning revealed the spiritual essence or soul-power of humans, animals, and earth. Words, too, were filled with this spiritual essence, materializing as breath vapors. A pledger of a sun dance used an eagle-bone whistle to direct breath prayers filled with his spiritual essence to eagle, Sun's messenger (Curtis 1970:75–76; Lowie 1935:319–20; Voget 1984:102–5, 211). The soul was like a shadowy conscious self, capable of leaving the body and moving about without restriction (Curtis 1970:53; Lowie 1935:69–71; cf. Hultkrantz 1953: 343–53).

The figure of a god who made all things indicates that the Crow, like their Hidatsa ancestors, were monotheists. Crow oral traditions and ethnographic literature do not always clearly indicate the Crow belief that the earth was created by an eternal, self-existing deity (Curtis 1970:52; Linderman 1931:13; Linderman 1962:79–80; Lowie 1935:251–53; Marquis 1974:134; Morgan 1959: 172; Nabokov 1970:302–3 n. 1: Wildschut 1975:1–2). A number of factors diverted Crow thought from a focused exploration of the nature of the Creator and his special place in their daily lives. For one thing, their daily existence was largely in the care of a spirit being or guardian with whom individuals maintained a close association. From their Hidatsa heritage they preserved a tradition of two creators who had shaped the earth from mud drawn from below floodwaters by a duck spirit and created its living inhabitants. First Worker and Lone Man were the Hidatsa co-creators, with First Worker the principal figure (Bowers 1965:298). The Crow developed two versions of the creation of the earth. In one, Sun and Old Man Coyote were the co-workers. In the other, Old Man Coyote and Little Coyote, or Little Fox, created the earth and its inhabitants (Linderman 1931: Lowie 1918:14–15).

The cunning and tricky behavior displayed by the Hidatsa First Worker when he bested Lone Man with his coyote transformation must have fascinated the Crow. Their favorite creator, Old Man Coyote, was a friendly, helpful, and lovable rascal whose image corresponded with that of the Hidatsa creator. In Crow mythology, Old Man Coyote frequently was referred to as First Worker (Lowie 1918:8, 34). A differential knowledge of oral traditions and differences in personal revelations led individuals to opposite interpretations and practices with regard to the sacred. People regularly prayed to Sun, according to White Arm, and never to Old Man Coyote. In One Blue Bead's judgment, "Old Man Coyote was the creator of everything—the equivalent of the white man's God (akbatat-dia), The Maker of Everything," while Sun was a secondary figure (Lowie 1935: 252). According to Two Leggings, First Worker had sent the Two Boys to teach the Crow about the Other Side Camp, which held the "same animals, birds, fishes, and plants . . . and the same rivers and . . . mountains" rising to the sky as were on earth (Nabokov 1970:25–28). Old Man Coyote was the chief of the Without Fires, the "two clans" of spirit persons of which the Other Side Camp was composed. Sun was "chief of all the sky beings" of the Without Fires, and the eagle was his "most important servant" (Nabokov 1970:25). When Two Leggings prayed, he invoked "First Worker, his medicine person, the sun, Bear Above, Great Above Person, and The One in the Sky" separately and in combination according to circumstances (Nabokov 1970:202 n. 1; Wildschut 1975:2).

The Medicine Quest

In an imperfect world filled with dangers of every kind, including hunger, sickness, and enemies intent on their elimination, Crow individually reached out for the spirit friends and protectors who, as the Creator promised, would respond to their cries for help. To prosper and survive, they needed to add to their own natural and sacred endowments the special powers with which spirit beings in all their diversity had been endowed by the Creator. These special powers could be observed in the flight of the eagle and the hawk and in their stealthy descent and grasp of prey. The otter, though small, was a tough fighter associated with water, and the buffalo and the bear showed the strength of their powers and capabilities to escape and recuperate when challenged by hunters.

Spirit persons owned their special powers and could transfer a right to their use to humans who came to them for help. Those seeking help were expected to show the extent of their need and sincerity of purpose by fasting without food and water and, at break of day, to offer flesh—a finger tip or joint, or small strips of skin. Acceptance of the flesh offering by a compassionate spirit person created a special bond between the two. The "medicine father" adopted the supplicant as his "medicine son" and conferred a right to his sacred power and the right to assemble talismans. During his lifetime a recipient of sacred power could dispose of his ownership right three times by adopting a medicine son. In any transfer of power by adoption, the recipient gave four things of value to his medicine father. Were a use-owner to dispose of his medicine a fourth time, the bond with his medicine father would be broken. Usually a man would retain one of the talismans of his medicine bundle to continue the relationship with his spirit patron (Linderman 1962:57–75; Lowie 1935:237–55; Nabokov 1970:22–27, 49–52; Wildschut 1975:43–46, 48–50, 53–54, 136–38). A man could add several sacred power rights to his natural endowment by fasting or by adoptive purchase. In any adoption the spirit patron had to be in agreement and confirm the transfer with vision or dream communications (Curtis 1970:54).

Crow usually sought the most powerful of spirit persons for their patrons. They found their patrons in the sky where spirit beings hurled lightning arrows and walked with moccasins ringed with fire (Wildschut 1975:48–50, 61–62). While visionaries might call upon the Creator to send them a strong Without Fires Person to partake of the flesh offering, Sun, because of his association with war, was petitioned as much as, if not more than, the Creator. Most gifts offered to spirit beings went to Sun. When Thomas H. Leforge and Bravo sweated prior to seeking a medicine father, their mentor "pricked flesh from . . . [their] arms and legs and gave it to the Sun" (Marquis 1974:132). Men and women validated their oaths by calling upon Sun to be their witness (Curtis 1970:69; Lowie 1935:217). When Leforge visited a former wife, then married to Cold Wind, she lifted up her hands and "solemnly invoked upon [him] the blessing of the Sun" (Marquis 1974:341).

Neither First Worker nor Sun was inclined to appear in

human form to fasters who prayed to them for help. Crow feared most stellar spirits because of those spirits' cannibalistic appetites and awesome powers, and Crow also feared that their Without Fires patrons sometimes gambled their lives away. Some, such as Moon, were better at gambling, while Sun was a noted loser (Nabokov 1970:26; cf. Lowie 1918:244–54). A man who received a power-vision from Sun enjoyed a rapid rise to fame and fortune, but he usually met an early death.

The Seven Bulls of the Great Dipper were especially friendly, for they served as guides of the night sky. Old Woman's Grandchild was a special hero of the night and morning sky. He was Sun's own son by a Hidatsa woman who had been lured into the sky world. After slaying monsters feeding on earth's living creatures, Old Woman's Grandchild retired to the heavens as Morning Star (Lowie 1918:52–74). Morning Star was the father of the twin heroes, Curtain and Spring Boy, who also prepared the earth for its living inhabitants by slaying monsters (Lowie 1918:74–98; Lowie 1935:112, 153–57). Crow also knew these twins as the Two Men.

When a man set out to "cry" for a spirit helper, he purified himself in body and in mind with a sacred sweat and commonly selected a location high in the mountains. There spirit helpers could come without fear of contaminants found in camp living. Eagle, Sun's powerful messenger, also dwelt in the mountains.

At his mountain retreat a faster arranged a bed of stones and cedar boughs so that Sun upon rising would brush his face. At the first sunrise, he offered his flesh in prayer to First Worker or to Grandfather Sun and asked that a Without Fires Person with strong medicine be sent to eat his flesh offering. He wanted power that would bring him wealth, speed and endurance in his horses, a

capability to sense the presence of enemies, and marriage to a woman of good family. A "medicine father"
could be expected on the second, fourth, or fifth day,
when a messenger bird alerted the suppliant's soul to
take note of the dress, talismans, songs, and body
painting displayed by his spirit patron. A medicine
father in the visitation appeared as a human being, but
on awakening at return of his soul, a faster usually
caught sight of an animal, bird, or flying insect and
knew that his patron was a Buffalo, Chicken Hawk, or
Dragonfly Person.

Crow sought medicine fathers represented by the
strongest animals and birds—such as buffalo, eagle,
hawk, otter, or grizzly bear—and rocks. Rocks suggest-
ing a buffalo, bear, or horse were used in hunting and in
horse raids, while rocks with human faces were especially powerful against enemies. Private medicines included a wide range of powers governing war, growth,
increase in numbers, movements of buffalo, weather,
curing, gambling, and a lover's feelings (Lowie 1922:
311–444; Lowie 1935:237–334; Wildschut 1975:1–173).

The medicine bundle based on private revelations
individualized Crow religion. During their lifetimes
men were in constant dialogue with spirit patrons
through dream communications in which they were
given special rights to obtain horses on an enemy raid,
to wrest a gun from an enemy, or to kill an enemy.
Women in their fasts during a time of mourning or
personal crisis received medicines, but they customarily
served as ceremonial assistants and caretakers of a husband's medicines. In essence, Crow religion was a family
worship in which a husband managed the sacred powers of his medicine bundle for his own personal needs
and the needs of family members, and occasionally for

community welfare. Private needs and community benefits met in public ceremonies, the initiative for which came from an individual instructed in a dream that he should sponsor a ceremony. The Crow could hold no public ceremony unless a spirit person desired it and communicated his wishes in a dream to an individual.

The Crow followed no calendar of public ceremonies, although a concern for the renewal of life and increase did lead them to correlate ceremonies with spring, summer, and fall. A medicine adoption established a "father" and "son" relationship, and each spring and fall during a full moon a man would commemorate that sacred bond by opening the bundle and speaking to his spiritual patron and the beings represented by the talismans.

Public Ceremonies

The Sacred Tobacco, Sun Dance, Cooked Meat Singing, and Bear Song Dance were the only ceremonies that required the cooperation of the public for their performance. The sponsor of a public ceremony obtained the consent of the band chief and elders well versed in the prophetic meaning of dreams, who made sure that the dream instructions were true and no evil would strike the community. Two other ceremonies, the Horse Dance and Medicine Pipe, were small associations of those who had purchased rights to sacred power by paying owners to adopt them (Lowie 1924:329–48). Satisfaction of personal needs was primary in Crow worship, and adoption was a basic procedure in the acquisition of sacred power essential to resolving human needs.

Members of the Tobacco Society planted seeds of the sacred tobacco every year when chokecherries were in bloom and harvested it when the fruit ripened. At any one time members were divided into four or five bundle groups, each originating in the vision experience of a founder. Weasel, Otter, Elk, White Bird, and Tobacco probably were the oldest of the Tobacco bundle groups or "chapters." (Curtis 1970:61–67; Denig 1985:188–93; Lowie 1919).

The Crow recorded the origins of sacred tobacco in favorite visionary themes in which a god or spirit person appeared to an orphan, a young man, a mourner, or an old man crying for a spirit for help. Sun, Morning Star, and the Seven Bulls of the Dipper usually appeared to the visionaries and gave them tobacco as a medicine. First Worker also gave tobacco to the first clay man he made (Curtis 1970:61–62; Denig 1985:188–93; Lowie 1918:14–15; Lowie 1920:176–89; Lowie 1935:274).

In its origin, tobacco came to be viewed as a medicine gift that distinguished the Crow as nomadic buffalo hunters from their hunting and cultivating Hidatsa ancestors (Bowers 1965:300–302). This found expression in the gift of tobacco to a younger Hidatsa brother, while the elder received a medicine pipe that bound him to the cultivation of corn and pumpkins. The same theme is echoed in the gift of a tobacco pod to one chief during a fast and the gift of corn to the other (Medicine Crow 1979a:66).

A popular tradition traced sacred tobacco to Chief No Vitals, who received it as a gift when fasting at a lake in North Dakota, now known as Devils Lake (Curtis 1970: 44–45). When No Vitals led the River Crow band westward, he took along the seven singers of the Tobacco ceremony. At the foot of the Big Horn Mountains he made the first planting, for Tobacco had shown himself there in the form of a shining star. Under Chief No

Vitals, sacred tobacco became part of the Crow's national destiny and heritage. At this first planting, Chief No Vitals cautioned them that as long as they shared the ceremonial planting, care, and powers of tobacco, they would become and remain a great people (Denig 1985: 189; Medicine Crow 1979a).

As in all Crow worship, tobacco signified the promise of good health, luck in war, and a long and productive life (Curtis 1970:61–67; Lowie 1919; Lowie 1935:274–96). However, tobacco was noted especially for the wealth it would generate. Tobacco seeds multiplied in the pods, and tobacco became a prime symbol of a numerical increase of any kind, in buffalo, horses, and humans. The ceremony consisted of a ceremonial planting in the spring, followed by the transmission of Tobacco medicines to candidates adopted into the bundle groups. Membership usually was by invitation, but a man might become a member by vowing to join were he successful in a horse raid or if he or a relative recovered from an illness. Adoption symbolized the birth of a child, and the ceremonial "father" and "mother" dressed thir "son" and "daughter" in new clothing. Their "children" reciprocated with lavish gifts, including horses. Adoption with payment formalized a candidate's right to acquire four Tobacco medicines, songs, and dances and to participate in the planting.

"Mixers" of the various chapters held rights to prepare the tobacco seeds and to supervise planting. The medicine dreams of mixers determined the location of the garden and the time of planting. A medicine woman led the procession to the garden, making four stops along the way to sing to the earth. She wore a wreath of ground cedar to drive away evil spirits bend on blocking their prayers and carried an Otter or Beaver medicine to ensure that the seedlings would have sufficient water to grow.

Before planting, each mixer started a warrior with a push on a run across the narrow width of the garden to stimulate and protect the growing plants. The run symbolized the path of a successful war party; on the return journey, the warrior would report that he had seen plenty of buffalo, groves of ripened berries, and tobacco seedlings pushing vigorously through the ground. Mixers initiated the planting by feinting three times before thrusting a painted chokecherry digging stick into the ground. Women imitated the mixer in their movements, while their husbands followed, dropping seeds in the holes. Before departing the garden, each chapter erected a miniature lodge in which Tobacco Man could sweat. Within it they burned Tobacco's bear root incense to assure him that they had followed sacred procedures. Throughout the ceremony they expressed the reverence and respect they felt for sacred tobacco and Morning Star, its owner.

The Sun Dance was a vengeance ceremony (Clark 1982:135–36; Curtis 1970:67–83; Lowie 1915; Lowie 1935: 297–326; Voget 1984:79–127). When a mourner in a vision or dream saw Sun's medicine tipi, he knew that, with that sacrifice, he would avenge a beloved relative slain by the enemy. Success, however, depended on proper guidance by an owner of a Sun Dance medicine bundle. A pledger also needed to get the consent of the head chief and wise elders, for this was the only Crow ceremony in which everyone was compelled to participate.

A Sun Dance (building a little tipi in imitation) took place in an enlarged tipi of twenty poles consecrated by a medicine man with power from Eagle, Sun's special messenger. The Crow looked upon the dance lodge as a sacrifice to Sun. War symbolism dominated the ceremonial building of the lodge. Trees were scouted as the enemy, and young men charged the first pole felled and counted wish-coups for guns and horses. A virtuous woman symbolically felled the tree by striking it with a wedge and blessed the revenge mission by calling upon Sun to bear witness that she had always been faithful to her husband. A captive woman, or a berdâche, felled the tree to weaken the heart of the enemy. War leaders consecrated the lodge with recitations of their military successes and gave dreams of dead enemies to the pledger. Young warriors reenacted their victorious skirmishes within the lodge.

The pledger danced on a white clay bed with eyes fixed on an effigy of the enemy. The little man was attached to a hoop ringed with eagle feathers, which hung in a freshly cut cedar tree. The cedar cleared the path of evil beings who might block the breath prayers pulsating from the pledger's eagle-bone whistle.

Young men took advantage of this medicine occasion to suspend themselves from lines dropped from the lodge poles to which they were attached by skewers inserted in their breasts. Others tried to dance loose from poles erected outside the lodge or pulled seven buffalo skulls attached with skewers to their backs. The pledger suffered no such torment but waited for the moment when, in his vision, the body of the little man would turn black. Black was a victor's color, and the pledger knew then that vengeance had been granted. The pledger's vision brought an end to his sacrifice and to the ceremony. All that remained was the departure of the avenging party and its victorious return. During the ceremony, mourners in the nearby hills cried and fasted for revenge and, on leaving the lodge site, left their flesh and finger-joint offerings in a willow bowl for Sun to eat. The pledger left fine mountain lion skins, a white buffalo hide, and eagle feathers for Sun.

Crow usually performed the Cooked Meat Singing and Bear Song Dance after a hard frost or snowfall to ensure a plentiful supply of food, good health, victories over enemies, and hearty growth in their population. The ceremonies expressed wishes that the Crow would get through the winter to the renewal of life in the spring without harm. The presence of Grizzly Bear was central to both ceremonies, although they were separate performances. In legend, Bear had been domesticated by Old Woman's Grandchild as a servant of his "grandmother" (Lowie 1935:140–41). Bear also was noted for his aggressive fighting and awesome invulnerability, as well as a capacity to recover from wounds.

The Cooked Meat Singing featured the medicines of mountain rock spirits. The fragmentation of rocks impressed the Crow as a wondrous capacity for an increase in numbers and of growth—a capacity also shared by the seed pods of sacred tobacco. Rocks that resembled buffalo, bears, horses, and humans were medicines to manage these animals and their populations and to deal with enemies as well (Lowie 1924:349–55; Lowie 1935: 258–63; Voget 1984:61–62; Wildschut 1975:98–103).

The fall, when yellow leaves dropped to the earth, was a perfect time for a medicine feast. Buffalo, deer, and elk offered fat and tender meat, and their hides were at their best for robes, tipi covers, and clothing. Mother Earth also displayed a bountiful harvest of berries and chokecherries for puddings and condiments. However, a sing could not take place until a medicine rock owner dreamt of bears. If a dreamer saw a bear eating chokecherries, he knew that he must host a sing as a feast giver, for chokecherries were important in making the sacred pemmican distributed in the ceremony. A host customarily invited ten well-known young warriors and their wives. Four of the ten would be renowned war captains. A host liked to invite a party of twenty, for that was a number sacred to Grizzly Bear.

The sing was a two-day ceremony, with the first day devoted to the preparation of pemmican and the consecration of a pemmican effigy of Bear. On the following night the host arranged a four-stage altar facing the mountains, which were visible through the door of the tipi. A chokecherry log draped with a beautifully tanned calfskin was first in line, then Bear's effigy, pemmican loaves, and a smudge fire of buffalo chips, bear root, and sweetgrass. Honored guests brought their rock medicines and smudged them before placing them on the calfskin.

The ceremony opened with a prayer during which an elder thrust a pointed stick into enemy eyes to the north, west, south, and east. Honored guests offered dream-prayers for the health and well-being of those present and for the Crow people, but the sharing of blessings as each owner sang to his medicine rock was a central element of the sing. On receiving his bundle, an owner unwrapped and pressed the medicine rock to his chest while making a prayer for good health and a happy long life. With an eagle wing in his left hand and a rattle in his right, he sang the four songs of his medicine with his wife as accompanist. As each singer completed his songs, he made a good-luck wish, touched the medicine with his lips, and passed it to the guest on his left, following the path Sun took in the heavens. During the circuit of the medicines, guests donated earrings, beads, feathers, and other wealth to the individual bundles.

No guest sang until he had given leather goods, robes, and even horses to the host. A singer and his wife also honored their respective paternal clan fathers with gifts, and these in turn protected them with dream-blessings. War captains alone offered medicine pipe prayers and recited coups. The fire was extinguished at this time, darkening the tipi in a re-creation of that singular moment when, alone in predawn darkness within a brush shelter, the war leader received confirmation of the promised victory over the enemy.

When the guests had sung to all the medicines, the host placed Bear's effigy at the doorway. A man with Bear medicine seated himself next to the effigy. He wore a rock medicine around his neck, and as he sang each of four medicine songs, he imitated a bear's call and stretched his hand toward the pemmican, palm down, in the traditional gesture when requesting a special favor. When the pipe lighter distributed the pemmican loaves, he squatted like an eagle and passed a loaf with his left hand to the guest to his right and used his right hand for a guest to his left. Sun was at the start of his morning path as host and guests shared a communion of pemmican in honor of Grizzly Bear.

The pledger of a Bear Song Dance usually had seen bears in his dream or had vowed to honor Bear in exchange for the cure of a wound or of a sickness. He killed a bear and for the ceremony attached the hide with claws to a cottonwood pole set in the ground. Bear dancers painted and dressed themselves in a tipi and then marched in single file toward the pole, with women in the lead and men following. One by one, as musicians drummed and sang four of Bear's songs, they were drawn to the pole. Each rubbed his face on the bearskin and then exhibited the medicine spirit within, represented by a horsetail, an egg, bear teeth, red paint, mud, and bird or buffalo tails. If the indwelling *batsirapay* spirit would not reenter a dancer's body, only the smoke of bear root or sweetgrass would bring him or her out of the trance (Lowie 1924:356–60; Lowie 1935:264–68).

The Bear Song Dance combined a theory of disease with the concept of a personal indwelling medicine spirit. Those with horsetails frequently suffered from rashes, boils, and other ailments that indicated that the *batsirapay* wanted to come out. However, those with horsetails also were noted for their wealth, while those with buffalo tails were expected to achieve reputations in doctoring wounds (Belden, cited in Lowie 1924:358).

The Sacred Order of Crow Society

Crow organized their society to ensure a safe transfer of sacred power that governed the well-being and success of individuals. In postcreation times, the spirit persons known as Two Men had demonstrated the procedure to the Hidatsa ancestors of the Crow. Paternal relatives were to use their gifts of sacred power to ensure the good health, wealth, and distinguished reputations of maternal relatives. Maternal relatives in return were to feast paternal relatives and to give them a portion of the bounty that paternal dream-blessings had earned for them.

Every Crow was born into a clan that traced descent through the mother. Clans guaranteed basic civil rights and obligated members to aid, revenge, and mourn each other as brothers and sisters. Clans also regulated marriage by directing members to select spouses from other clans. During the nineteenth century, Crow clans numbered twelve or thirteen, with two or three clans forming cooperative bonds for hunting, mutual aid, and feasting.

Crow formalized the bond between a father's and a mother's clan by emphasizing that a person belonged to his mother's clan but was a "child" of the father's maternal clan. Paternal relatives, grandparents excepted, were singled out for deferential respect by treating a father's maternal line as if all were fathers or mothers, even to an infant in a cradleboard. Children whose fathers were of the same clan formed a group of "teasing relatives" who kept each other in line by making sure that foolish mistakes received a public airing (Frey 1987; Lowie 1935:18–31, passim; Voget 1984:32–37; Voget 1987:207–16).

Reciprocities uniting a father's and a mother's clan began at infancy when a paternal clansman was asked to pierce a "child's" ears and to name him. When the boy walked, the "clan father" went to the family with a halter to claim a horse in payment for his protective blessing. When a boy killed his first deer or buffalo calf, the time had arrived for clan fathers to direct their sacred powers to advance the career of their clan child. Beginning with the hunter's art, the sweat lodge served as the stage for launching a child's career. Clan fathers went to the lodge on invitation to sweat and pray for their child, and four took special dream wishes. Two wishes promised health and life. A dream of ripened berries protected the child until late summer, and a vision of an old man with a wrinkled face promised old age. The giveaway was the vehicle of repayment. Maternal relatives distributed horses, buffalo robes, leggings, moccasins, and other wealth to clan fathers and mothers. A giveaway also honored a child with public recognition of his achievement and the discharge of responsibilities to clan fathers, to whom a large part of his success was owed.

As a young man began his career as a horse raider and warrior, the dreams of clan fathers might convey rights to a gun taken from an enemy, a horse slipped from its hobbles inside the enemy camp, or an enemy scalp. Four standard coups measured the success of individual warriors and their religious and political influence. To become well known, a warrior was expected to wrest a weapon from an enemy, to be first to strike a coup with a weapon or coup stick, to ride away with a horse tethered before an enemy tipi, and to lead a successful war party without losing a man to the enemy. He then became an acknowledged war captain with the right to carry a medicine pipe on his expeditions, and his achievements readied him for advancement to chief of the band.

Throughout his career a Crow warrior maintained a constant discourse with spiritual beings through his medicine bundle, fasting, sweating, and dreaming. In the Sacred Sweat he prayed to all the powerful spirit persons. He poured four buffalo-horn spoons of water on the hot stones for Sun, seven for the Seven Bulls of the Dipper, ten for Morning Star, and an uncounted number for the myriad Star Persons who shone forth at night. Warriors personified sacred power, and the Crow took no personal or community action without a warrior reciting a coup and wishing success. With medicine pipe and tobacco in the hands of a renowned warrior, the Crow could be assured that spirit persons at the Four Winds, Star Persons above, and earth's Without Fires People were always close by.

The hunt, warfare, and a personal search for a medicine father formalized a progressive development for boys that was lacking for girls. Women achieved their reputations largely through their domestic skills, the bearing of children, and their devotion and faithfulness to their husbands. Faithfulness earned a woman an honored role in public ceremonies, such as the Sun Dance. Without public career incentives, girls simply acquired craft and domestic skills by following the leads of their mothers and left the ascent of mountains and fasting for a friendly spirit helper to young men. They were reminded, too, that male spirit helpers, following Morning Star's lead, commonly took fright and departed when confronted with female reproductive effluents (Lowie 1935:151–57). This antithesis between female functions and the masculine sacred did not lead to a rite of passage that celebrated the menarche as a positive acquisition of medicine. In the sacred order of things, men learned how to handle medicines from their spirit patrons, and women served as their assistants and as custodians of the medicines when in camp and on the march.

Women did acquire personal medicines but usually through inheritance or a spirit visitation when fasting during mourning or because of a personal crisis. Woman Chief was a notable exception to the domesticity expected of women. She was an Atsina captured around 1816 when she was about ten years of age. Her captor encouraged her inclinations to learn how to hunt and to shoot with bow and arrow and gun. According to fur trader Edwin Denig (1985:196), "Long before she had ventured on the war path she could rival any of the young men in all their amusements and occupations, was a capital shot with the rifle, and would spend most of her time in killing deer and bighorn, which she butchered and carried home on her back when hunting on foot. At other times she joined in the surround on horse, could kill four or five buffalo at a race, cut up the animals without assistance, and bring the meat and hides home." Denig (1930:433) described her as completely fearless, attacking and killing grizzly bears when alone. Her war exploits, which earned her a third-rank seat among the chiefs in council, were equally daring. She killed and scalped a Blackfeet warrior, counted first coup, wrested a gun from the enemy, and also led war parties with success. While maintaining the life-style of a chief with guns, lances, war horses, and four wives, she continued to dress as a woman. Denig, however, said nothing about medicine—whether she owed her charmed life to a medicine acquired through a traditional fast or adoption by a renowned warrior, or whether she had been naturally endowed without a visitation.

Rigid distinctions separating men and women in their personalities and activities did not encourage women to lay claim to medicines men used in the hunt and in war. One Child Woman went out to fast because she felt neglected by her husband. He loved to gamble, and One Child Woman may have feared that he would wager her away, as men sometimes did with their wives. By fasting she hoped to attract the attention of a spirit person who would help her; then she saw an object shining in the distance. The shiny stone had to be a medicine, for it had four faces, one of which resembled her husband, while the others suggested a buffalo, an eagle, and a horse. She took the medicine rock to her father, but when she told her husband of the find, he went immediately to his father-in-law's tipi and removed the stone. Through the rock's powers and the dreams he received, One Child Woman's husband abandoned gambling as a career and became a rich and famous warrior, well known for his dream prophecies (Wildschut 1975:105–7).

In a world dominated by dangers of the hunt and of war, the wish-dreams of "clan mothers" undoubtedly contributed to the successes of their "clan children."

Clan mothers and fathers (today's clan aunts and uncles) equally were rewarded at giveaways with gifts of horses, robes, and leatherwork. The close association of women with reproduction, nurturance, growth, and population increase gave them a prominent ceremonial role in the planting of sacred tobacco and in the Cooked Meat Singing. Medicine women generally worked with herbs, as those who cured colic with tobacco plugs and applied tobacco juices to cuts and aches (Voget, field notes). Some followed a common procedure of medicine men and sucked the "bad stuff" from the patient with a pipestem, while others drew upon the powers of bear or buffalo for a cure (Linderman 1972:112; Lowie 1935:62–64). Older women usually served as midwives for a relative but called in a medicine woman with a root to ease delivery if difficulties arose (Linderman 1972:145–49; Lowie 1935:33).

Crow Reservation Culture

Reciprocities linking a father's and a mother's clan to the transfer of medicine constituted the core of Crow culture and served as the foundation of Crow reservation culture. Interclan reciprocities were solidly grounded because they formed an economic system of mutual benefits shared by intermarrying families and their immediate bloodlines.

Destruction of the buffalo and the shift to a reservation life left young men and women in a state of social limbo. Young men especially could not achieve social reputations and wealth in the old ways, and the agency infrastructure was too shallow to provide the incentives, training, knowledge, and physical resources to bridge to a new way of farming and ranching.

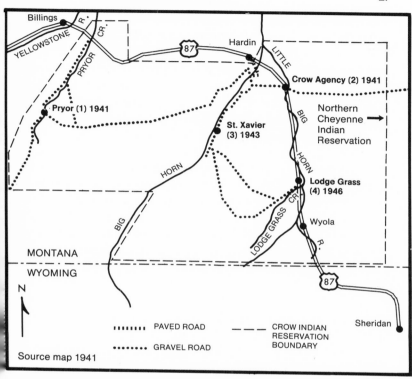

Map 2. Crow Indian Reservation, 1941. Numbers in parentheses indicate sequence of district sponsorship of the Shoshoni Sun Dance after its introduction to the Crow in 1941.

The Crow in the meantime set to work to fill the vacuum in their lives by importing ceremonies and dances that offered status positions that could be acquired through adoption and purchase. Within their own religious and ceremonial system they also intensified the purchase of rights and the exchange of wealth through adoption (Medicine Crow 1939). This was especially true of the Tobacco ceremony (Lowie 1935:276–79).

Crow reservation culture received its infusion of new status ceremonies from the 1870s to around 1920, some of which were social and some religious. During this period of status elaboration, the Crow invented the so-called trotting or push dance, adapted from the fox-trot, and the shaking hands dance to end the New Year's Dance, borrowing on the handshaking practices of Christians and, perhaps, Indian Shakers from the Pacific Northwest.

A compromise arrangement with the agent around 1910 led the Crow to interweave their own ceremonies and social get-togethers with a year-round calendar of events celebrated on Christian and government holidays. This calendar stabilized Crow reservation culture. It provided legitimate occasions for the Crow to dress, sing, dance, and hold giveaways in accordance with their own traditions, even though modifications were necessary for lack of proper material, social, or sacred resources. The new arrangement ended a ban on dancing and feasting put into effect by the commissioner of Indian affairs in 1902 (Bradley 1972:175–80).

For their reservation giveaways the Crow were forced to find substitutes that would match the beauty and quality of gifts exchanged in buffalo-hunting days. There was no substitute for a gift of a horse, but a costly and colorful Pendleton blanket could serve in place of the quilled, beaded, and painted buffalo robes in which Crow wrapped themselves. Woolen blankets and comforters covered wooden floors or bedsprings in clapboard or log houses in place of buffalo-hide comforters used as bedding in tipis. Beaded moccasins, gloves, and belts were not always made of locally tanned deer and elk hides, but the lavish beadwork with the traditional light blue background added style to any dancer's costume. The money tree was a special invention for the giveaway. Twenty or thirty one-dollar bills were attached to a leafy chokecherry bough for distribution to one or more paternal clan uncles (Voget 1990).

Interfamily reciprocities promoting the welfare of a "clan child" contributed a special flexibility to Crow reservation culture (Voget 1987:207–14). The Crow were able to incorporate selectively the content of American culture without seriously disturbing the foundations of their own way of life. The blessings and medicine tokens of clan uncles and aunts influenced the play of individual basketball players and the winning of district championships, all of which required giveaways to repay clan uncles and aunts and to honor the players. Occasions for a "giving thanks" giveaway ranged over all manner of personal achievements, including school honors, scholarships, top athlete awards, making the game-winning basket, selection as beauty queen, election to tribal or public office, and recovery from illness. Wars also kept alive the image of the warrior as the primary giver of blessings at public ceremonies. Crow servicemen commonly carried medicine feathers obtained from paternal clan uncles to help them succeed and to protect them from harm. A giveaway marked both the departure and the return of Crow soldiers, and Soldier Boys' Day was incorporated into the calendar round in 1918 for servicemen to honor and reward their clan uncles and aunts.

The introduction of Christian missions during the late nineteenth and early twentieth centuries both challenged and stimulated the spiritual base of the reservation culture. Although converts to the Baptist, Catholic, and Congregational faiths were urged to abandon their medicines, medicine bundles survived among families with renowned Rock, Arrow, and Tobacco medicines.

Church membership did not mean a wholehearted con-
version to the Christian way. Medicine pipes continued
to circulate among fireside gatherings of neighborly
church members, who offered puffs of tobacco to spirits
standing forth as shining points of light in the night sky.
Medicine men continued to cure church members by
sucking out the "bad stuff" with cylindrical stone pipes
and ashwood pipestems. Church membership also was
no bar to participation in giveaway reciprocities.

The spiritual heritage of historic Crow culture guided
the formation and elaboration of the reservation culture
from about 1910 to 1945. While Christian churches
expanded missionary and educational activities, the
Crow in 1910 added the Peyote religion to their reservation culture (Kiste n.d.; Stewart 1987:184–89). Peyote was
not a bundle ceremony, but, following the old way, it did
invite participation by individuals as they felt a need.
Although moral reform was possible through Peyote, it
was more a way of curing. Peyote provided the oppor-
tunity for personal communication with the Creator, or
a spirit person, through a vision experience and a
chance to sing one's devotion in the old way with drum,
rattle, and feathered staff. Worshippers also could pray
with tobacco wrapped in the form of cigarettes. Aimee
Semple McPherson's claim to curing powers led to the
introduction of the Foursquare Gospel in the 1930s. In
1941, some sixty-six years after the last performance of a
Crow Sun Dance, William Big Day, with the aid of a
Shoshoni Sun Dance leader, introduced the Shoshoni
Sun Dance to the Crow (Voget 1984:129–47). Shoshoni
medicines distributed by John Trehero reasserted the
primacy of the traditional medicine bundle over the
Peyote religion and Christianity in obtaining and manag-

ing spiritual power in the curing of diseases and in the enjoyment of good-luck blessings and wealth.

Today the face and fabric of Crow reservation culture has changed considerably from that of the childhood of Donnie and Agnes Deernose. The horse-and-buggy visiting of the Crow began to decline during the 1930s with the introduction of the automobile. Real changes, however, began soon after World War II when status relationships of men and women began to alter as women became more independent in family, political, and religious affairs. The status of veterans as primary prayer givers gradually gave way to the selection of individuals according to character and civil achievements. When women entered the Sun Dance as dancers, rather than as fasters in the traditional way, they enhanced their status as individuals possessing sacred power to use for the benefit of others. Women frequently are invited to bless dancers who are their "clan children" before they leave the lodge.

Church, school, and sports provided opportunities for both boys and girls to achieve special awards for which they could be honored with a giveaway. Girls serve as cheerleaders at basketball games, but they have yet to be honored as a team because they have not won a championship, as the high school boys have done. To be first is reason enough for a giveaway, as happened in 1968 when a young girl was the first Crow to join a Catholic Order.

Since World War II, the second generation of Crow born on the reservation, as grandparents, have been unable to transmit the Crow heritage locked up in warriors' exploits, legends, and oral histories to the succeeding generation of teenagers. Young people today are drifting away from their Crow heritage and increasingly ignore and ridicule formal rules governing kin behavior. Cars, sports, school, television, and good times projected by American teenage culture claim their attention, and with their rock music cassettes they are tuning out both Crow values and language.

Economic conditions prevailing on the reservation and widespread change have steadily eroded the status of males, but clan uncles still are preferred in the naming and blessing of a clan child, whether boy or girl. Veterans are the preferred choice to bless the center pole of the Sun Dance lodge and of the ceremony generally. Clan uncles usually furnish the medicines for basketball players, arrow throwers, and teammates in the gambling competition known as "hiding."

While seepages from the outside world continue to undermine Crow reservation culture, the greatest challenge is from within. Crow converts to evangelical Christianity, Pentecostals in particular, have separated themselves from the giveaway and the traditional religious bonds and reciprocities that have produced continuities in Crow culture. The many participants of the Shoshoni-Crow Sun Dance and of Peyote demonstrate the deep reservoir of feeling that supports the view of the sacred as medicine and associated interfamily and interclan reciprocities. Introduction in 1986 of the Sioux Sun Dance,in which votaries use skewers for suspension and flesh offerings for prayer, adds further support to the traditional religious orientation and practices. The Crow, however, appear to be at a turning point, as they are dividing into two religious groups, followers of traditional worship and evangelical Christians.

The founding of Little Big Horn College in 1980 provided opportunities for Crow youth to develop an awareness of their history and experience a pride in their cultural heritage. Two-thirds of the faculty are Crow. Under President Janine Pease-Windy Boy, the college developed an associate of arts degree in Crow studies. Courses include the Crow language, oral literature, family and kinship, history of the chiefs, and art, music, and dance. Students are introduced to personal and general issues relating to Indian identity, social problems of the reservation, and American Indian values, thought, and philosophy. Relations with federal and state governments are covered by courses in tribal government, Indian law, and development of reservation resources and economy. Neither the Crow culture studies nor the bilingual program have arrested a decline in Crow speakers, which now is estimated at less than 35 percent.

Crow history in the past was retained largely in personal and family anecdotal histories and in public knowledge of outstanding chiefs, hunts, battles, and ceremonial performances. Crow are preserving their present-day history and culture with family narratives, photographs, and audio-visual recordings of public events for deposit in their archives. Professors Joe Medicine Crow and Dale Old Horn, together with Dr. Barney Old Coyote, have striven to establish Crow oral tradition as authentic history and as a measure of the factual accuracy and interpretation of historic and ethnographic accounts. Oral traditions also have been used to describe historic events as Indians experienced them, such as the Battle of the Little Big Horn, and the tactics that defeated Custer (Kammen, Lefthand, and Marshall 1992).

The appointment of Joe Medicine Crow as tribal historian and anthropologist in 1948 signaled the beginning of a deepening interest by the Crow people in their own history. In the years that followed, Crow authors produced a number of works relating to Crow history, culture, culture change, and vignettes of daily life. The new historic orientation prompted development of a more comprehensive view of Crow relations with the federal and state governments and their place in the politics, and economies of town, county, and state. To secure their measure of political representation, Crow leaders organized voters, and in court action challenged entrenched voting procedures that denied Crow majorities legitimate representation. Through their political activism the Crow have elected a county commissioner, a county sheriff, a state representative, and a senator.

CHAPTER 2

I'm Born a Crow Indian

My Birth in a Tent

I was told that I began my life in a tent during our Crow Indian Fair held in October at Crow Agency in 1908. My folks were camped out in a tipi made of canvas. They moved to the fairgrounds and pitched their tipi across from the agency on October 26th, and I was born the next day. There was a hospital right across the way, but in those days Crows didn't like to go to the hospital. They called the hospital "the sick peoples' lodge," and it was a strange place from which you might not come out alive. Most kids began their lives in a tent the way I did, and when they got sick, they usually were doctored at home by a medicine man.

Once I was on the way, my mother put herself under the guidance of her mother, as old people knew what to do. They had beliefs in the old days that if a woman slept with her feet facing a doorway, she would have an easy time of it. To sleep with her feet toward a wall in a tipi, or a log house, would make it hard for the baby to come out. Crows also didn't like a woman to stand or sit with her backside to a fire because that heat held back the afterbirth and might cause her to die.

Mother had to get herself up at sunrise and had to drink plenty of water and soup. Each time she took water she rubbed her abdomen to keep me from getting stuck, and she walked a lot to keep me down to size. They didn't have many nine- or ten-pound babies in those days. Mother also made sure not to lift anything heavy, and she didn't do any heavy work at all for about ten days before I was to arrive. As for my father, he didn't go hunting because he knew that his shot would miss the deer anyway. That's the way it is for hunters even today when a wife is in a family way. There is something mysterious that comes between the hunter and the animal so the hunter can't shoot straight.

In the old days when a baby was born in a tipi, whoever was attending the pregnant woman put up two sturdy poles at the place where a wife rested her head when sleeping. She would kneel on soft skins (especially buffalo robes), rest her elbows on the pillow, and grasp the stout poles. Once the baby was born, getting the afterbirth out was the big problem. No men or boys could be present at childbirth, for they would make it even harder on the woman. So the father-to-be would go and stay with a brother or a married sister. Some older woman, who in a dream had received a special medicine to make birth easier, was asked to take charge. She always had to be paid with something valuable, maybe a horse. A mother and grandmother usually were present, and the grandmother might be the one to cut the umbilical cord, which was measured at three fingers in breadth from the navel.

After the child was born, the older women took the buffalo robe with the afterbirth to a brushy area some distance from the camp. They drained the blood off and raised the robe four times to make the child grow. Crows always do things four times in a ritual way. Any blood that happened to get on the floor of the tipi was scraped up and thrown away outside the camp, and new dirt was brought in and the area then was smoked with sage. When everything had been cleaned up inside the tipi, the woman's mother smoked it with running cedar, fir needles, and bear root, if that was the husband's medicine. Then the tipi was fully purified and was ready for the father's return.

Although I was an old-fashioned baby, I was born in a tent, not a tipi. During early reservation days they shifted the birth to a tent instead of a tipi or log house. My sister, Amy, told me that she and my cousin played in the tent the family put up for my birth. They had a bed ready for my mother, and she could have used those poles, just as in the old days. My mother's younger sister, Mary Takes The Gun, acted as a midwife, for she was like a medicine woman and knew a lot.

In the old days the Crow women washed a newborn with water, but in my time they greased the infant with olive oil and then wiped it off. That's what my mother's sister did with me. Then she wrapped me in a blanket and brought me to my mother's bed, which was in the tipi. When my father came to see me, he called on his own mother to bring me for him to see. He didn't take me in his arms, but he did want to know if I looked like him. My father couldn't ask my mother's mother to bring me to him because he could not talk to his mother-in-law, and she couldn't talk to him either.

Mother didn't nurse me until the third day, for she did not have milk until then. My family brought in a woman who was nursing. She dropped a few drops of milk into my mouth to start me sucking. In the old days Crow women used to bring a two-week-old puppy to suck a first-time mother's nipples if they were not large enough or properly formed. Sometimes even with the second child they would get a puppy to bring on a good flow of milk.

By the time my mother began nursing me, my grandmother had pierced my ears. Crows often did it right away when first wrapping the newborn, but in my case I was two days old. Some used to wait until the fourth day. My father's mother heated the end of a metal awl to keep the blood from flowing and pierced my ears in three different places. Then she took a very small piece of the heartwood of the yellow willow, greased it, and placed it in the hole. Yellow willow was best because the wood was naturally smooth. When I was a few weeks old, my mother knew it was time to remove the willow piece form the bottom hole and to insert a small blue shell brought from the Pacific Coast. Boys got off easier than girls with their ears, and usually they had only one hole, or maybe two. Crows continued piercing girls' ears on the third or fourth day until the thirties. Nowadays girls get their ears pierced when they want to, and I don't know of any boys who have their ears pierced.

I slept with my mother's mother at first, for they were afraid my mother might roll over and smother me. Whenever I cried out of hunger, Grandma would take me to my mother and then carry me back to her bed. They didn't let me sleep with my mother until I was sitting up when I was about five months old. After that, my sleeping time was divided between a grandmother and Mother, but I came to like sleeping with my father's mother the best. She used to rock me to sleep, and when I first awakened, she whispered "tch, tch, tch" in my ears and then she sang lullabies to me. She sang one song about a colt running with his mane waving, and of his large ears and twitching tail. She also sang about the parts of a rabbit that people ate: the choice tripe, kidneys, and even the little balls. And every time they put me to bed at night, my grandmother used running cedar to smoke the house to drive away any evil spirits who might be around. Some people used bear root, or *eseh*, as we call it. People used a different smoke according to their medicine, but cedar is one they usually use to make sure that their prayers get through.

Protecting the Newborn

Crows always were fearful that a baby or a youngster would get sick, especially with pneumonia. If that happened, they called in a medicine man who was known for his cures. He used an ash or chokecherry tube to suck out the bad stuff, and he usually received a horse and several comforters as payment. When I was about six years old, I took sick with double pneumonia, and my parents took me to an Indian doctor by the name of Gros Ventre. My mother said I was just skin and bones by then. He sucked all the bad blood out and cured me. In those days Indian doctors were great. They could do almost anything and even could put bones together. People always tried to pay them well with four things, for the cure worked better with the spirit helpers that way. And that's the way it works today, too, if you go to a medicine man for a cure. For four things today, Crows like to give a Pendleton blanket, dress goods, tobacco, and money.

People always wanted the newborn to grow and to get tall, and so they wouldn't let anyone step over it. If some boy or girl happened to step over a baby or a growing child, the grown-ups made them step back again. Even when grown up you were not supposed to step over someone. When the Crow were moving around in the old days and came to a spring where a spirit person lived, a mother would give her infant, or young child, some beads or tobacco to throw in there so that the infant would grow to manhood or womanhood. They used to do that at a warm spring near Livingston by Yellowstone Park and at Big Spring, north of Pryor. The mother spoke to the "person" in the spring by saying, "I want this boy (or girl) to grow up to be a man (or woman)."

Medicine dreams were protective of the infant and growing child. This is where our paternal relatives come in. They dream our growth, life, and success for us. Losing a first child always was bad luck for a couple. When this happened, a man and his wife often went into the nearby hills to fast together for four days, and they often mourned for three months or more. Sometimes when they fasted, the man or the woman might receive a vision-message from a spirit person with instructions to make a necklace or other thing to keep the newborn in good health. Crows tell of one man who lost two boys in succession. In his fasting he happened to walk among some prairie dog holes, and finally he sat down. He dreamed of a large prairie dog hole, and out of it came lots of girls. Each one had a blue and white bead necklace to which two elk teeth were attached. Besides the usual braid at each side, some of the girls had another small braid on the left side, others a small braid at the back. After that, the man had five daughters. He fixed a necklace of blue and white beads for each one of them when they were ready to start walking, for the girls he saw in his dream walked out of the prairie dog hole. All five of the girls had long lives. When a man or woman had such a medicine, others came to him or her for help so that their children might grow up healthy. But the

parents or grandparents had to give the person something of value for such a medicine-blessing, usually a
horse. A horse was our best gift and our standard
measure of wealth. A horse is still the best gift today,
and brothers-in-law usually save to give horses to each
other. These are not just ordinary horses but racehorses
with papers. They do that because there is a special
respect relationship between brothers-in-law and between sisters-in-law, too.

To protect their newborn, the Crow people also used a
name-blessing that could bring good health and pros-
perity to the child. They invited a man known to have
powers (usually an outstanding warrior, and often a
clansman of the father), to give a name-blessing at the
time when the ears were pierced. This usually was done
for a boy child. After the naming the father would invite
his clan brothers to a feast, and these men would tell of
their dreams. Their summer dreams always looked
ahead to winter when snow was on the ground, and
their winter dreams always looked ahead to the time
when the grass was green and it was warm. That is how
they protected their children from year to year with
dream-blessings. An Indian name given by a clan uncle
or a well-known clan brother is still considered important to the health and the success of Crow children.

If a child, after getting a name, turned out to be sickly,
a medicine man would be called to change the name.
When Cuts The Bear's Ears, a medicine man, named a
boy one time, he painted the boy's face yellow with two
red spots on his cheeks. He then raised the boy four
times, smoking him with cedar incense, and named him
High Cedar. "Here is High Cedar," he said, "and you
who are present will never hear someone say that he has
passed away. He will live to an old age." And that's the

way it turned out. Every morning for ten years the father painted the boy's face yellow with the two red spots and prayed with tobacco that the boy would grow up healthy. He stopped the painting when High Cedar didn't want to be different from other boys of his age.

They had another way of curing a child who was sick a lot. If the parents worried that the child might die, they might make him a "throwaway" child. The parents would take a sick infant to a prearranged spot and a close friend or a relative, usually a clan aunt or uncle, would take the child home. The new parents blessed the infant and gave him a new name and new clothes. This was like a rebirth, and the new parents were now considered to be the child's real father and mother. The new mother and father were always concerned about the welfare of their child even though he might not live with them. Parents told an older child that what they were doing was a blessing wish that he get a new start, grow up strong, and become well-known. A "throwaway" child might get well right away, or it might take a longer time. By custom, the new father and mother were given four gifts, usually Pendleton blankets, three or four quilts, money, and cigarettes, and sometimes a horse.

Some children had their names changed as many as three or more times. Boys were more sickly than girls, so they had their names changed more often. Names were connected to luck and to wealth, and that is another reason boys had their names changed more often.

A medicine necklace or a medicine tied to the back of the head was usual for boys, while girls had a small braid on the left side where a medicine bead or a shell might be attached. You don't see those medicine braids much any more, but quite a few children still wear medicine necklaces to protect their health.

Taking Care of a New Mother

Mother said she didn't have much time to rest after I was born. They wouldn't let her do any cooking or work for about ten days, but my two grandmothers made her get up and walk to prevent blood poisoning. They also saw to it that she drank plenty of water and soup to produce milk. My mother said she could never seem to get enough to eat. She wanted to eat all the time, not just in the morning and evening as the Crow were used to doing. My father's mother was especially fond of natural vegetables and fruits, and she would go out in the morning and bring back wild turnips, twin grass, chokecherries, and berries for making soup when she could find them. Mother never lost her appetite for meat either, and she sucked on dried meat dipped in meat soup to increase her supply of milk. In the old days the Crow had this milkweed that they soaked in warm water. When the water turned green, the nursing mother would drink it, sipping some of it off and on all day. This never failed. Sometimes the gummy substance the plant gave out would be chewed, but you had to break up many stalks to get enough gum to chew. Nowadays rice is often used along with regular or evaporated milk to make a good flow of milk. Beef soup is also a favorite, but now most kids grow up with a bottle, especially if they are adopted.

Cradles, Colic, and Weaning

I spent my early days on a cradleboard. My father's mother made my cradleboard. In the Crow way, the father's side should do this, either his mother or his sister. Father had a sister, but his mother wanted to do it.

I was laced into my cradleboard with my arms at my sides and only my face showing. My family was still using powdered dust from rotting wood and red paint powder to help keep me dry and free from chafing and itching. Pieces of cloth soaked up my soil in place of soft hide, or my mother slipped a kind of pillow made of hide and stuffed with pine needles under me. Crows were still using that kind of pillow when Joe Medicine Crow was a baby around 1914.

My mother was a great tanner of hides, and when she went back to work in about ten days she could have given me a cow's teat to suck on to keep me quiet, for the original pacifier had been a buffalo's teat. Mothers used to give young ones some of that tough gristle from the brisket to suck on and also let them suck on the chokecherry stick used to dig marrow from the bones or used in making berry puddings. Chokecherry was good because it didn't splinter like other woods. Of course, mothers used to feed their babies just about every time the infants cried, and they always left open part of the sleeve under the arm for nursing. That's the way I did it when nursing Bobby. I never heard what my family did with my umbilical cord when it fell off. In the old days Crows sewed it up in a beaded piece and tied it to the cradleboard.

Whenever they took me out of the cradleboard for rest and play, Father liked to raise me up and bounce me on his knee and give me a kiss on the cheek. When I started to sit up, around the fifth month, and showed an interest in crawling, it was time to take me out of the cradleboard. When I was able to sit up I played with a stick with a string of beads attached to it, or I was given a tin cup to knock around. Waving my arms up and down jiggled the beads and kept me quiet for a while, which was what my mother and grandmother wanted. When I started to crawl, they had to watch me all the time to make sure I didn't get burned on the kitchen stove.

Colic was a common problem for babies. In the old days there always were old women who were specialists in "ass ache," as colic was called. Some mothers and grandmothers were big chewers of tobacco, while the men rolled cigarettes out of Bull Durham tobacco. Colic specialists would grease the backside of the baby and slip a wad of chewed tobacco up there. If that didn't work, they'd take a big pot and fill it with cold water. Then they'd put the colicky baby in the water, usually waist high. They'd leave him in the cold water until he stopped crying; then they wrapped the baby in a warm skin or blanket, and he usually went right to sleep. My sister, Amy, used to do that with her baby, Joe Medicine Crow, and it worked.

Colic wasn't the only remedy the old women used chewing tobacco for. If you had sore legs, they'd rub it on, and it helped take out the ache. They also put it on cuts and then wrapped them up. Not many women of my generation took up tobacco chewing, and chewing went out pretty much with the old-timers in the forties.

When I began to make more talking sounds, Grandma Stays By The Water tried to teach me a few words, like *papa, mama,* and *give me.* She was my constant nurse-maid. At our house, wooden benches and Grandmother's knees helped me to stand up, and before long I took my first steps, reaching for outstretched arms. I was about a year old when I first walked. Father sent word to the clan uncle who had named me that "his child was walking." When my clan uncle came, he brought along a lariat, sang his "glad song" for my success, and then claimed the horse owed for his good-luck blessing. Mothers were proud of children who walked early, but I didn't walk early enough for my mother to brag about. The first steps were very important, because it meant that a walking baby was on his way, protected by dream-blessings of his clan uncles. It showed they had powerful medicines for their "child."

Weaning was not a happy time, and a baby always wanted to go to the mother for food. Mother and Grandmother tried to plan ahead. Sometimes when Mother was eating and holding me in her lap, she would slip a piece of fat to me. That was around the fourth month when my lower cutting teeth made their appearance. They started me out on a watery soup, and gradually I got less water, more soup, and less breast milk. When it looked like I could take straight soup and eat solid foods with my baby teeth, Mother took some black from inside a tobacco pipe and smeared it on her nipples. That bad taste started me to crying. This happened before I began to walk. Once they began the soup-and-water diet, I was always hungry, and Grandma had to pack me around on her back, walking most of the time to keep me quiet. I used to get her up some nights, and she would have to walk and walk. Then, when they broke me with that tobacco blackening, Grandma had to do her walking at her own place, for every time I saw my mother I would cry out to be breast-fed. Crow mothers don't use that tobacco black any more. My sister, Amy, and I didn't use it either, but we fed our babies milk out of a cup and spooned in soft foods. Our mother and grandmothers were always there to help out, and even today a grandma's back is the preferred carryall for babies. In my mother's time, and even during my childhood, mothers used to nurse kids that were two and three years old and running around and playing.

Dressing Up in White Clothes

In the old days Crows dressed boys of two to three years in moccasins, hip-length leggings, and a breechcloth of soft hide. Girls wore moccasins, short leggings, and a short buckskin dress gathered at the middle with a belt. After I began to walk, I wore a simple calico dress that ended just below my knees. Little boys, especially in summer, wore a little outer shirt that barely covered the crotch. There wasn't much of the old-style dress around when I was growing up because hides for tanning were hard to get, even though the men still hunted elk and deer.

Some men, when they began to wear pants, had the seat cut out so the legs were like leggings and they could wear a cloth breechcloth. My mother cut and made dresses for herself and us girls from dress goods, and this was common for women into the thirties. During the late thirties and forties, Crows worked for wages in the WPA (Works Progress Administration) and also at jobs during the war. I think that money helped girls become more style-conscious and started them to buy dresses at the store.

Church and school had a lot to do with getting us into white man's clothes. You had to look nice when you went to church and to school. We had to give up our moccasins and put on high-topped shoes. Boys entering the government boarding school in Crow Agency had their braids cut off and wore a military uniform with a jacket, trousers, black shoes, and a round black hat. The school had the girls wear gingham dresses with the same design on so they would all look alike, too.

It wasn't like that at our Baptist mission school where I went. The mission gave out dresses, pants, shoes, socks,

and underclothing sent free from people in the East. We
all took what fitted best, and our mothers and grandmothers altered them to fit. In those days people didn't
always know what they should wear to church, and Dr.
Petzoldt (Baptist minister) used to tell how one well-
known Crow warrior turned up at church one Sunday
dressed in shoes, long underwear, and a high hat. He
always liked to tell that story because it seemed so funny
to him.

CHAPTER 3

My Family and Relatives

I'm a Yellowtail

My father's name was Yellowtail, Epaysheedush in Crow. His real name was Hawk With The Yellow Tail. He had no family name or first name, only an Indian name, for that was our way. His father was Bull That Rises Up, and his mother was Stays By The Water. She was of the Big-lodge clan, and because of his mother, my father was a Big-lodge member. My mother was a Whistling-water, and that's the clan I belong to, Bedekyosha. They made us change to the White ways, and so taking the name of my father as my last name, I was born a Yellowtail. We have kept our way of naming, and my Indian or honor name is Comes Out Of The Water. People don't use their Indian names except on important occasions. My common name you might say is Agnes.

When I was a young lady (*beagata*), I began to learn about the clan by going to where the Bedekyosha were holding a sham battle or giveaway. I learned that Crows were not supposed to marry someone from their own clan. That's why my father, a Big-lodge, married a Whistling-water. All members of your own clan were considered to be your relatives, even though they weren't really; you couldn't marry anyone who was your relative.

The Big-lodge people did, and they were the worst ones to marry into their own clan.

Today people aren't as strict about marrying into their own clans, but in my day there would be much talk, and your teasing relatives would make real fun of you in public. I don't know how that teasing came about. Making fun of a person in public kept you in line. We waited our turn to get back at our joking relatives because you weren't supposed to get mad when they teased you. We still tease, but ties between the father's and mother's clansmen are loosening, and the joking between children whose fathers are of the same clan is not like it used to be. I got my teasing relatives from my dad's Big-lodge clan.

Clan marriages sometimes led to some funny situations. My husband, Donnie, belonged to the same clan as my father. That meant that I was Donnie's "clan child" and should address him as "father" and respect him just like my real father. it was the same way with my brother-in-law, John Whiteman, who married my sister, Amy. He was a Big-lodge, too, and so Amy was his "child" and so was I. Donnie and John used to tease us both about it, referring to us as their children and saying they'd have to watch how we behaved. Actually, in real life and in public, I called my husband by his name, Donnie. I don't know whether marrying into one's own clan is good or bad. Anyway, it doesn't seem to matter anymore.

When I was growing up, you were supposed to respect clan uncles and aunts on your father's side. All men and boys of a father's bloodline (matrilineage) were like "fathers," even to babes-in-arms. We also respected all the women of the father's line by calling them "mother." In showing respect you were expected to help them all you could by making them feel good, giving them some money, and never passing them by without saying something good. In return they wished you luck and good health. When you were older, a boy or girl of your own clan was not expected to show you the same respect they gave to a clan uncle or aunt. It was up to them if they wanted to do something nice for you.

The Yellowtails and the Shoshoni Washakies

In a bloodline way, the Yellowtails are related to the Shoshoni of Wyoming through their famous chief Washakie. The Mountain Crow band used to winter around the Wind River Mountains in Wyoming. They scattered themselves in small groups, and sometimes they ran into Chief Washakie and the Shoshonis, and a fight would break out. That's what happened one time, and we're related because Chief Washakie made off with Bull That Rises Up's sister and married her. The way the story goes, Rises Up and his sister and mother were getting ready to flee, as the fighting did not go well for the Crow. The sister was on a horse, and her mother was standing, holding the reins. Rises Up was alongside of them. A Shoshoni rode right between them and pulled the reins out of his mother's hand and took off with the sister in tow. They could hear her crying as the rest of the people began to flee. Rises Up's mother told him, "Rises Up, you are a big boy and have a fast horse. Ride and catch up with the rest of them. I'm going to follow your sister." She caught up with the Shoshoni man, who turned out to be Chief Washakie himself. He must have been a mean man, for he married the sister, even though she was only fifteen years old. Charlie Washakie was their oldest child. The mother and daughter never returned to the Crows.

I never knew Charlie Washakie and my Shoshoni relatives until I was a young woman. Our families visited back and forth. Charlie's wife was a white lady, light-skinned with reddish hair, but she was the best Indian ever! She always dressed like an Indian. When she passed away, they sent for us, and at her funeral I saw that they had dressed her as a white person.

My Family

My mother was not a full-blooded Indian and never had an Indian name. People called her "Dayshay," but I think that was their way of saying "Lizzie." She had French in her and looked more white than Indian. Her hair was light and not black like the Indians, and she always had the appearance of a white woman in Indian dress. She also had blue eyes.

Mother's father was known as Frenchie, with a last name of Frazee. He married Emma, the daughter of Pierre Chienne (also D'Chienne, Duchien) and Bear In The Woods. Mother and her younger sister, Mary, were brought up by their grandparents and were enrolled under the name of Chienne. Neither Mother nor Mary went to school, for in those days they didn't believe in going to school just to learn English. A chance came, but the grandmother didn't want the girls to leave because she needed them to help out with the work. Mary did learn to speak a little English, but the best that Mother could muster was a few words.

In those days they were not very strict in marrying, and Frenchie had two wives: my grandmother Emma and another wife in Canada. He trapped a little and took Grandma with him to help out, and then he took his furs to Canada where he lived with his wife for about three months. We found all this out after my grandmother passed away. Frenchie left a large family in Canada, and my mother got to see one of her Canadian relatives who was over ninety when he passed away.

During my grandmother's time, Crow men frequently had two wives. They liked to marry sisters since sisters got along better than wives who were not related. When a man was killed on the warpath, a brother could take the widow as a wife, even though he already was married. It was our custom, too, that when a maternal uncle passed away, a sister's son could take his widow as a wife. A woman really wan't free to marry anyone she wanted after her man passed away. Her man and his relatives had given horses and other wealth for her, and so they still could claim her. All that has changed now, but when I married Donnie is 1931, there were several men who were married to two women. Usually the wives lived in separate districts. The missionaries were much against those marriages and worked with the law to break them up.

In my family there were three boys and two girls. Of the boys, Robbie and Carson were older, and Tom was the youngest. My brothers and my sister, Amy, went to a government boarding school at Crow Agency. Robbie soon was sent away to Riverside, California, and he never returned until he graduated six years later. Tom went away to Bacone, a Baptist college in Muskogee, Oklahoma. He finished the sixth grade and then quit school to get married. His best schoolmate and friend at Bacone was Pete Lefthand, but that's the way classmates were supposed to be. They're like brothers to each other. Carson quit school early to get married, too, something that happened to most boys and girls in my time. My sister, Amy, was too sick to get much education at the boarding school, and my mother wouldn't let me get much because she needed me at home and wanted me to marry early. That was the way for girls in the old days, and they wouldn't get in trouble this way and bring shame on their brothers. I myself didn't get past the seventh grade, and I dropped out when I was sixteen years old because my folks forced me to get married.

Robbie got the best education of any of us, and he is really well educated. He has farmed and raised cattle, but he made his mark in politics, doing many good things for his people. When he was just a young man, he was sent as a delegate to Washington, D.C. There was a movement afoot to turn our reservation loose and open it up to the Whites. Robbie fought it and so we have our reservation today. He was superintendent of the Crow for four years.

The government built a dam on the Big Horn Canyon and named it after him, even though he opposed it. To this day he doesn't understand why they decided to call it the Yellowtail Dam. Back in 1956, building the dam divided us into the Mountain Crow Club and the River Crow Club. These names were taken from Crow bands of the old days, but on the dam issue they were nothing more than nicknames. Crows like to poke fun with names, and they like to get some good laughs at the expense of their opponents. The Mountain Crow bunch was named because they wanted to preserve a mountainous area near the damsite that was a kind of animal refuge and held mineral and timber wealth. It was a kind of sacred area, too, this Big Horn Canyon. The River Crow bunch got their name because they favored the dam. The Mountain Crow bunch were afraid that the wording of the contract would allow the government at a later time to take over more land than was needed for the

The Yellowtail family around 1930. Left to right: Tom, Carson, Robert, Lizzie, May, and Agnes. Courtesy Hardin Photo Service.

dam. But the River Crow had the backing of the Hardin Chamber of Commerce and other important people, and the Mountain Crow lost.

George Hogan, Jr., the son of Robbie's maternal uncle, led a movement to change the name of the Yellowtail Dam, and they did change the name of the lake made by the dam from Yellowtail Lake to Big Horn Lake. Among the Crow a maternal uncle is a very special person. He is like an older brother, and we call him "older brother." An "older brother" is supposed to watch over you, advise you, and help you out. His son is like a son to you. That's why it was a big surprise and hurt Robbie when his "son" joined the other side and was active in the naming, too.

Robbie was married four times. Two of his wives died, and he separated from one. He doesn't farm anymore, but he still has cattle. He is ninety years old now and still rides horseback. Robbie was baptized by the Congregational minister, Burgess, while he was in the boarding school at Crow Agency. There hasn't been a Congregational church on the reservation since the Baptists bought them out around 1920. Robbie goes to the Baptist mission church and also to all six churches in Lodge Grass. He puts in his offering and tells how he was baptized and became a church member. He still is a politician today.

Father had no schooling, but he wanted us to go to school. He used to say, "Things are going to change. As you grow older, there's going to be lots of change." He was a quiet, dependable, and well-respected man. Whatever he set out to do, he did well. He and Mother worked hard for everything they had. Like other Crow men in those days, he counted his wealth in horses, and he had a lot of horses. He was a good man who taught us never to steal or to tell a lie. He taught us kids in a nice way, never scolding or raising his voice. I think that was why we listened to him more than to anyone else. I was always waiting for him to come home, and he was the only one who could make me stop crying. I was the youngest and a terrible kid! Picking me up, Father would say, "Listen, I hear a coyote crying!" I'd listen and stop, and then I'd start crying again. Again he'd say, "Listen!" I'd stop, and then I'd realize that I was the coyote. Another way he'd get me to stop was by tickling. He'd say, "I'm going to count how many ribs this little girl has." He'd count in Crow — *hawatgat, dubeh, shobeh* — and when he got below my arm, he'd make me laugh. He had more patience with me, and at times my sister, Amy, would have liked to kill me. I guess you could say that I was a spoiled kid at that age, and my parents were the ones who did it. You can see why I came to feel real close to my father, more than to my mother.

Father was a very religious man. When I was growing up, he used to tell us once a year that he was going down into the brush where no animals had stomped the ground. There he would build a little sweat lodge. I sometimes followed him there, but he wanted to be alone with the Maker Of Everything, the one we now call Akbatatdea. I imagine he prayed to the Creator to look after his family. After he came home, I would get curious and sneak down there to see. It was a real little sweat lodge, and as he built it, he must have prayed. Crows in the old belief always prayed when they were building a place for worship, like a sweat lodge, or a Sun Dance lodge, and people still do that today.

Before the old people ever did anything important, they prayed for a good-luck blessing. They wanted the spirit persons to know what they were doing and that

Agnes's father, Hawk With The Yellow Tail, Yellowtail. Courtesy Hardin Photo Service.

they prayed for the help of the spirit persons. Of course, you had to be willing and ready to give something good in return for their blessings. This was the way my father believed and worshipped before he became a Christian, a Baptist, as my mother and we children were; he never completely gave it up.

My father must have been about sixty when his health began to fail, something with his stomach. My mother's sister, Mary Takes The Gun, sent him to an Indian doctor in Canada. That was around 1922 or 1924. Mary had heard about this Indian doctor sometime before and had brought him to Crow Agency, where he doctored quite a few Indians. I think he was a Stony Indian, or what you call an Assiniboin.

To get money for the train ticket to Canada, my father sold two palomino horses to Nelson Storm, a man from Denmark who manned the railroad section house. Storm had no use for the horses but gave two hundred dollars for them to help out. He was a good neighbor. Three others went along. There was Mortimer Plenty-hawk, who was sick with tuberculosis; Joe Not Afraid, who had a heart condition; and Billy Steals, Joe's adopted father, who went along just to be with his "son."

The Indian doctor had a white dirt as his medicine, which he put into water to find out what was going to happen. When he came to my father, he said, "When I put this dirt in the water, if it spreads out, you will get well right away. If it does not spread out, the sickness will be hard to cure." When the doctor put in the medicine dirt, father saw that it didn't spread out. It was going to take some time for him to get well. When it was Billy Steals's turn, he said, "No, I don't want to be doctored. I'm not sick."

When they got back, Joe and Mortimer got well right

away, but it took a while for my father to get back on his feet. Billy Steals, who didn't want to be doctored, was the first to pass away.

The Indian doctor gave my father some of his medicine powder, a few tablespoonsful, and my father tied it up in a buckskin. Only a little was needed. If a cloud, like a tornado, came up, you could make a little cross with this medicine powder on the forehead of each family member. Then outside you would get down on your knees and pray, and the bad storm would not hurt anyone. One day a cloud came that looked real bad — pink, green, and blue. As a child I always was afraid of storms, and so I called to my father, "Come and use that medicine, so the storm will go away." He painted us on our foreheads, and we went down into the storage cellar while Father went out to pray. Sure enough, the storm didn't hurt us but went around us.

In the old days, a father was the real head of the family because he was the main provider of food and the protector of the family. Through his fasting and prayers he was given power to do great things. A man and his wife were like a spiritual team, but while a woman might fast and receive some medicine, the man was the main one.

My father followed the ancient Tobacco veneration of the Crow. Sometimes he would get a Tobacco medicine song in his sleep and would wake up singing. As a kid I was a light sleeper, and I'd hear his song. In the morning when he sang his song, I'd sing right along with him. He'd exclaim, *"He-haa shodaje?* How does it happen that this girl knows that song?" I know some of his songs today and have some songs of my own. Like my father, I was adopted into the Tobacco Society, and so was my sister, Amy. Sometimes when they have the Tobacco adoption, I hear songs that belonged to my father. When they adopt you, or make you reborn, they give you four different medicine songs and four medicines. Four different people usually give them. You don't get the medicines for nothing. You must give four valuable things to those who adopt you and to those who give you the medicines and songs. Right now my brother-in-law wants to use some of my songs, but he hasn't given me anything yet, so I haven't let him use them.

Fathers and Mothers on the Reservation

Life on the reservation was real hard on our men because they no longer could be fathers in the Crow way, and they couldn't become well-known persons in the old way. With the passing of the buffalo and of wars against our Lakota, Piegan, Cheyenne, and Arapaho enemies, our men were no longer able to bring food and wealth by hunting and raiding for horses. The older men, the chiefs, had made it in the old way, and their stories of hunts and war parties, and their images of success, carried over into the dreams of our younger men. As a child I can remember how sporty young men dressed out in fancy boots and spurs with pistols locked into their broad leather belts. My brother-in-law was one of them. And do you know who dressed them out in these fancy clothes? Their in-laws, for that was always part of the marriage exchange. The groom's parents and relatives in turn dressed up a daughter-in-law.

Firing guns was always a part of our festivities in those days, especially by winners of horse races and by warriors dramatizing the return of war parties. That firing during the Crow Fair used to really scare us kids, and we'd run and hide behind our grandmas or in the tipis.

With wars, the Yellow Eyes kept alive the image of the warrior with mysterious power. Some of our young men led war parties in World War II and are judged by some to be like chiefs of the old days. Our last old-time chief was Plenty Coups, who died in 1932.

Today a veteran is called to mark with black rings the forked cottonwood tree used as a center pole in the Sun Dance. He tells the crier about his success against the Iron Hats or the Wolf Men (Japanese), and the crier relays it to the people. Black was our victory color during the buffalo-hunting days. Warriors of a victorious war party mixed buffalo blood and charcoal to blacken their faces and clothing to show the coups they had struck on the enemy.

Food was hard to get after the government stopped giving out rations. Men brought in meat seasonally when hunting elk or deer in the Big Horn Mountains, and women continued to prepare the food, dress the skins, and make clothing as in the old days. The idea that women should put the food on the table was carried over, and women had to dig deep into their money purses and work hard at drying fruits and Indian turnips to keep hunger away.

Men and women in the old days had their own properties, and neither could tell the other what to do with his or her stuff. The main properties for men were horses, horse gear, guns, and medicine, while women owned the food, tipi, and household things. This ownership idea continued, and each kept control over his lease money when White ranchers paid up. If a man bought a car, he didn't like to get help from his wife. Even though she had only five dollars in the car, she could say "No!" when her husband wanted to lend the car to a friend. It worked the same way for women who wanted to be free to use their lease money to buy what they wanted. Children also had their property rights. Of course, when a father and mother had a giveaway for their child, the father usually paid for some of the blankets and dress goods. Some men also helped out with food and clothing and household things.

Getting a start at ranching was always hard because it took about ten acres to feed each cow, and you needed about two hundred head. Most allotments were for eighty or one hundred and sixty acres, and White inheritance rules made it harder by dividing it into smaller pieces with lots of heirs. Leasing to Whites was the only way to make use of our lands, although some Crows kept a few cattle for food and for a donation to a feast.

When I was growing up, we still considered men to be heads of the families, and I always told my son and my grandchildren that Donnie, my second husband, was the head of our family. I did that so they would have respect for him. Today it seems like women are becoming the heads of the families. Some are in politics, holding tribal offices, and quite a few have danced in the Sun Dance right along with the men. In religious matters, women always were supporters of the men. But it's different now. I guess you could say that education, church, and women's lib have changed women's attitudes.

We are still a family-oriented people and hate to get far away from our relatives and friends. When away from our loved ones, we may dream of them. If we dream that they are in an accident, we get on the phone right away, so they can pray and dodge that bad thing. The old way is to go to the river and offer a smoke-prayer with tobacco and to throw the clothing seen in the dream into the river. That way the evil will be carried away and nothing will happen, especially if you cut off some of your hair and throw it into the river, too.

Although we love to be at home on the reservation, it is not big enough to take care of everyone in an economic way. Our young men excel at sports, especially basketball. Many carry medicine feathers on loan from clan uncles to help them make baskets. Outstanding players and winning teams are honored with giveaways. Most of the blankets, shawls, money, and horses given go to the clan uncles of a player, for they have made him a success with their medicine-dreams, and they have to be paid back.

Basketball and graduation honors give a good start to our young men and women. But when players leave high school they have few chances to make good at a job on the reservation, and they can't find the way to a happy and good life. It's hard to make it in the city, and many don't like to leave their families and friends. Too many of our young men turn to alcohol and now to drugs. Perhaps I should not say it, but it seems as if all the bad things that come to us are given by the Yellow Eyes.

CHAPTER 4

Growing Up

Starting Life with an Indian Name

Soon after I was born, a clan uncle gave me a special Indian name with a blessing to keep me strong and healthy. My father always called me by that Indian name, Bahosay-hayday-awaajish, Sits Among The Cattails.

Today I use my public or honor name, Comes Out Of The Water, Bedah-ko-wasaadua. That is how I am known among the Crow. My father's sister, who was my clan aunt, married a Hidatsa Indian, and after she died, he stayed with us. My clan aunt was a kind of mother, and she looked out for me and did everything to make me happy when I went to her place. Her husband's name was Long Bull, and his English name was Adlai, just like Adlai Stevenson. He took the place of my clan aunt after she died and watched out for me, and he gave me good things. He became pretty well known and paid money to my aunt's sister, Mrs. Don't Mix, for the name, Comes Out Of The Water. After Long Bull paid for the name, he had it announced at a dance that he was giving me the name. This made it legal in our way. My name refers to the red-winged blackbirds that nest in swampy places and fly out of the water.

If you need a name for public use, you always begin with your clan uncles and aunts, since you have the right to buy a name that they own. They may offer it to you, but you have to give them something for it. Once my brother Robbie gave one of his names, Summer, to his Big-lodge clan child. It was at a political meeting, and Robbie and his clan child were on opposite sides of the question. I think Robbie decided to give him the name to stop the opposition. When he announced the gift, clan relatives dug into their pockets to pay something to Robbie on the spot. A clan child is not supposed to show any disrespect to a clan uncle and should never criticize him in public.

Grandparents, Grandchildren, and Adoptions

Our family never was made up of just Father, Mother, and us kids. Father's half-brother, Robert Rises Up, lived with us after his wife died. Mother took care of him until he passed away. Crows very often take in a relative who has lost a spouse. My mother used to keep her sister's boys, Frank and George Takes The Gun. My brother Robbie's daughter Joy stayed with us. She was two years younger than I was.

As a kid you never could count on growing up in your own family. Crows have always adopted children. I imagine it started with the hardships of our buffalo-hunting and war days. When a young mother with children lost her husband, she let grandparents or an older sister take over their care. In my own case, my older sister, Amy, spoke for my first and only child, Bobby. I was separated from my husband, and she knew I was single and could not take care of him. I had no job, lived with my parents, and was dependent on lease money, which I got only once a year. For these reasons she offered to take care of him. My sister also warned me that if I wanted to get married again, my next husband would not like to have a stepchild. I agreed then, but I now think that some men could accept stepchildren and be good to them. When Donnie and I married, we had an understanding that his child would be like mine, and mine would be just like his. When Bobby came back from the army and married Clara, Donnie treated him as his own child. He also adopted Duane, our first grandson. We took him at nine months to wean from his mother, and we have kept him ever since. Donnie thought the world of Duane. It was the same when we took in my maternal uncle's children, Ataloa and Ferale Hogan, after their mother died.

George Hogan was my mother's brother, and he was like an older brother to me in the Crow way. When my mother adopted Ataloa, she became a younger sister to me. And when I adopted Ferale as my daughter, she became a granddaughter to my mother.

This habit of adopting grandchildren continues right to the present day. During early days on the reservation, adoption papers were not needed. Grandparents, or whoever adopted a child, drew the lease money and got use of the land that belonged to the child. If an adopted child died before he grew up to claim his money and land, the land went to the adoptive parents. It was their way to earn a little extra money, for life was not easy. In turn, the adopted child would inherit land from the grandparents, or from the one who adopted him. Women were the ones who usually were on the lookout for a child to adopt. Crows often called their adopted grandchildren *aworaybeh*, which is like a treasure found.

Grandparents always took the oldest child for adoption. That's why my father's mother, Stays By The Water, took Robbie when he was four years old. In a way she

On the way to get buffalo for the Crow tribal herd, near Yellowstone Park, 1934. Left to right, seated: Lizzie Yellowtail, Ataloa (adopted daughter of Lizzie), Winona Plenty Hoops, and Maggie (wife of Robert Yellowtail). Left to right, standing: Young Yellow Wolf, Walks Over The Ice, Lester Jefferson, Robert Yellowtail, and Robert Howe. Courtesy Hardin Photo Service.

adopted not only Robbie, but me and Tom also. Later Tom was adopted by my mother's mother, Emma Chienne. Her husband, One Star, adopted my sister, Amy.

I was lucky to have two grandmas nearby to visit, for they always had good things around to eat. My father's mother lived with us, while my mother's mother lived about a mile away across the railroad tracks where my sister and her husband, John Whiteman, now live. I often went to my maternal grandma's place where I'd play for a couple of hours and then make the dust fly as I ran home. I couldn't have been more than five years old, and I remember how they always told me to stop and watch for the trains. There was no road then, and we had no White neighbors except for Nelson Storm at the railroad section house. He lived alone and always liked to have us drop by to talk.

Because of adoption, you usually didn't grow up with your own brothers and sisters. My sister, Amy, was ten years old when Grandma Emma and One Star took her for adoption. Grandma would bring Amy every day to visit, for Crows like to share children. They don't think of adoption as giving a child up. When adopted by grandparents, a child usually inherited their lands. Emma Chienne left her land to One Star, her husband. When he died, Amy got all of it, as he had adopted her and her son, Joe Medicine Crow.

My father's mother, Stays By The Water, was always taking us on horseback to dig roots and to pick berries. She was a lot of fun and had a beautiful voice. When parents invited the clan uncles to bless a "child," they always invited her, and she sang praise songs for the children. When she sang her praise song, you could hear her all over the camp. She became well known among the people.

Amy, Agnes's sister. Courtesy Hardin Photo Service

When I was old enough to go to school, Stays By The Water used to hide me from the Indian police because she didn't want me to go to school. This was true of many other Crow parents and grandparents. The Indian police acted as truant officers, and they were mean, even to their own people. That was the time Big Medicine headed the police. Grandma and I would go out into the hills and dig wild turnips all day. We rode horseback, and one time we went up a coulee where there was a cool spring. She told me that she used to hide my brother Robbie there when they were going to put him in the government school at Crow Agency. Once while we were at the coulee spring, our horses startled and a rider came up. It was Robbie, who was living up in the mountains at that time. He wondered what we were doing there, and Grandma reminded him of the times she had hidden him from the police.

Grandma Stays By The Water used to take us children to the ice cream stand and buy us cones. She also bought shoes and clothes for me with her lease money. I can remember the first pair of shoes she bought for me. She wanted to get me high-top shoes with laces, but I wanted pretty slippers. She finally let me have my way. We were at the shopping almost the whole day, and I wanted to get back and show off the slippers. But when I put them on, my mother was very angry and asked Grandma why she had bought those slippers. Grandma said that she would fix them, and fix them she did. She cut the tops off a pair of high-topped shoes and sewed them on, and I wore those shoes to school. Little girls liked to dress like their older sisters and mothers, and I was no different. When I asked my mother for a shawl so I could look as good as my friends, she gave me a fringed tablecloth. I didn't know any better and wore it, and I can still see my schoolmates cupping their hands over their mouths in the Crow way and giggling.

Home Life

Our house was located about three miles south of Lodge Grass. At first we had a big one-room log house with a dirt floor, but when they closed down Fort Custer in 1906, Father got some boards and added another big room. Mother used to water the dirt floor over and over again, making it real hard. We slept on the dirt floor on top of rugs. Later on Mother got a single iron bed with iron springs, and for a time I slept with her. She always put a lot of blankets on the bed, and it was very cozy. But all good things end, and when I was about four years old, I began sleeping on the floor, making my bed at the head end of my mother and father's bed. I was afraid because they scared me with stories about Red Woman and how she would get me. That's why I wanted to sleep close to them.

We had a wood and coal stove but burned wood mostly. Father used to get some coal from the freight train when it was stopped at the Little Horn section house. He climbed up and threw the coal down, and the train men didn't seem to mind. Sometimes they even threw chunks of coal down to him. After throwing down the coal, he came home, hitched up his team, and went after it. That was a big help, for we didn't have to buy coal and fuel when other people were short. Living was cheaper then, for there were no electric bills and no need to buy gas for a car.

My brother Robbie now lives in the old house, although it has changed some from my childhood. In those days, all of our houses had the back door opening to the east, and that was the door we used. Houses were built with a front door facing west, but Crows never finished them with a porch or stairs. Winds blow mostly from the west and north, so it was better to have the door on the east side of the house. In the old days Crows always pitched the tipis to the east so they could greet the Sun with their prayers when they came out into the daylight.

In my time, when you passed a house, there was a wall-type tent or a canvas-covered tipi pitched nearby. People didn't like to live in houses and spent as much time as possible outside in tents. The air was fresher, and tents were cooler during the day because you could roll them up just like the Crow used to roll up the buffalo-hide covers of tipis in the old days. When the days started to shorten up and get cold, the tent always heated up faster under the sun.

We had another house, a log winter house. Father built it close to Lodge Grass, right over the hill from where we now live. He built it on land that belonged to his mother, Stays By The Water. Her land ran over the hill and just a little ways over Lodge Grass Creek and made up eighty acres. As soon as it started to get cold, they moved us kids over there with Grandma, who kept house for us and got us off to school. Mother and Father would get wood in for the winter, about ten loads for our winter house and the same for the main house. It was slow work because wagons were not very big and did not hold much. They moved us into the winter house around the first of December, and by March the weather was good enough for us to return to the main house and ride our horses to school from there. Quite a few families built along Lodge Grass Creek because they didn't want their kids to ride too far to school in the cold. On some days it was a good thirty degrees below zero, and the wind was icy. The little community along Lodge Grass Creek came to be called Muddy Mouth, Eshebea in Crow.

In the evening we kids could not run around and make much noise in the house because every night father would smoke a peace pipe and pray. When father had a visitor, mother used to keep us quiet by telling us stories, and sometimes she would tell us a White man's story or legend. At other times we would lie down on the floor with our friends and take turns telling stories instead of chasing each other around. We told stories about horses, beavers, coyotes, and birds. There was a good one about a mouse, too. Grandma Stays By The Water told us many of these stories, and she also sang lullabies that told us about the different animals and their habits.

Old men used to get together regularly in the evening to smoke and pray. When we were living in our winter house, Pete Lefthand's grandfather, Bird Tail That Rattles, would come over every evening. He was a Sioux and lived just a little ways from us. George No Horse came often, too. The men always sat toward the back and the women and kids up by the door. This was the way it was in the old days in the tipi. The place of honor, and the place where a man hung his medicine, was in the back of the tipi. Here he received his guests, and whatever they had to do together, they first opened with a smoke-prayer. When Father and Bird Tail That Rattles smoked, they pointed the pipe to the Star People and to Mother Earth and the Earth People. Each one would say, "You, whoever is up there, take a puff." Then they pointed to where the winds came from, first the north, then the south, and said the same thing. I never saw them go to the east or west with the pipe. I think this tobacco smoking to the stars and cold and warm winds was meant to take care of everything, to keep us strong and healthy and to protect us from harm during the winter.

When Mary Takes The Gun, my mother's sister, came to visit, she used to burn cedar, which had green berries. When it was smoking, she would take it into every room to drive away all the evil spirits and keep them away. She always prayed when smoking the room. I use that cedar myself once in a while, even today. Mother's sister, who was like my other mother, used those green berries from the cedar as her aspirin to take away pains in the head, legs, and arms. It was good and really worked. Today cedar is used in all ceremonies, including the Sun Dance, to drive away evil spirits that might interfere with prayers or harm people.

Kids were around the old people a lot, and we learned to respect them and what they were doing and saying. When they were smoking and praying, they were pretty strict, and we were not allowed to walk in front of them but had to pass around at the back. We noticed how the old men would make a circuit to the left of the stove when they were leaving, the same as they used to do when leaving the tipi. I think kids today would be smart if they listened more to older people and learned from them. Now, young people are busy running around in cars, and they don't want to listen or pay attention to older people.

Play

The house, the tent, and the river were where we played when we weren't at school. With only horses and buggies and hardly any roads, people just couldn't take off at any time and run to the neighbor's place or go to town.

Girls usually played together because brothers and sisters were not supposed to play together and boys made fun of any boy who played with girls. They'd tease him: "You must be part girl." If a boy played a lot with girls, he might even get something, like his knee might swell up. So boys stayed away from girls pretty much in their play. I never played with my brother Tom at school, only at home. In the case of the Carpenter girls, they had a younger brother to take care of, so he had to play with us girls.

Brothers and sisters in the Crow way were not supposed to touch each other once they got to be around six or seven years of age. We were getting to be young ladies then and were no longer little girls, or *beagatgata*. Brothers and sisters were taught early to respect each other. After they grew up, a brother would not enter a house to talk with his sister if she was alone. Even after I was married, my brother Robbie used to drive up and toot the horn. If I was home alone, I'd come out to his car to talk to him there. In wagons and later in cars, a brother never sat next to his sister. Someone was always in between, or the brother and sister were separated in the front and back seats. Crow brothers and sisters still do not sit next to each other, and when they go to a show they sit apart with friends if they can. I like it that way.

We used to laugh at the way White brothers and sisters wrestled and hit each other and even held hands. But now some Crow brothers and sisters fight and argue with each other just like the White kids.

When I was five years old, we practically lived in the water during the hot days of summer. Our neighbors, the Carpenters, lived across the Little Big Horn from us. Mary, Mary Ann, Philomene, and their little brother, Joe, waded the river to get to our place. We'd swim all day.

When we got too cold, we'd run back to the tent by the house. The tent was hot, and we'd cover ourselves with blankets to warm up and play at sweating. Finally, one of us would cry out, "It's hot, let's go swimming again!" And away we'd run to the river.

We liked to play house, making a little tipi with little beds. We made mud pies and pretended we were cooking with dishes. Our rag dolls had a head made of cloth wadding. We never added any arms or legs, but we did make sleeves. We pulled threads from a piece of cloth to give our dolls a fringed shawl. We gave up playing tipi when we were changing into little women, about eight or nine years of age. I never played with my older sister, Amy, except for the time she brought us a big box of dishes and dolls. She was eleven years older than I. She made the dolls from little pieces of buckskin to which she sewed some beads. All of these dolls are gone now.

I had so much fun playing with the Carpenter kids that I always made plans with them for the next day. If we played hide-and-seek until it got dark, they were scared to go home, and so either Father would ride horseback and take them home or their grandfather would come for them.

We rode horseback a lot. Two or three of us would ride one horse. In chasing other riders, one of us always would start to fall off, and in hanging on to each other, we'd all fall off. It was hard for us to climb back on the horse, for we had no saddles.

Foot racing was another fun game for us. We used to get my father's mother to start us and see who won. She would wait until we were ready and then say, *"Naawada!"* — "Now go!" or "Charge!" — and she would laugh and laugh at us as we ran. Men used that *"Naawada!"* when they charged the enemy. Father's brother, Moccasin Top, lived over the hill behind Lodge Grass Creek at Eshebea. He was a "father" to me, and his children were my "brothers" and "sisters." When they went to the store in Lodge Grass, they would come by for a visit. One of my "sisters," Isabel, was a fast runner. We always raced against her, hoping to win, but she was too fast, and not even the boys could beat her.

At school we picked up some games from the White kids. Kick-the-can was a favorite, and so was hide-and-seek. During recess, we played Annie-over, throwing a ball over the roof of the schoolhouse, and if we caught the ball, we'd sneak around and try to capture one of the other team players by hitting or touching her with the ball. We also jumped rope, counting the times until a person missed. We always counted and spoke in Crow because we didn't know much English then.

Boys brought marbles and played with pocketknives. Mumblety-peg, which we called knife-in-the-ground-hits *(bechea-mapa-chewok)*, always drew a circle of admiring watchers, for some of the boys were very good. They never bet, which surprises me now, for Crows have always enjoyed betting. We always bet at our horse races, arrow throwing, and the hand game. We have intertribal hand game tournaments now.

Miracle Stories, Red Woman, and Owls

As children, when Tom and I came in from playing, we sometimes would tell stories to each other and sing lullabies. But we liked best of all to get Mother and Father to tell stories. Sometimes during the storytelling Mother would make buffalo or serviceberry pudding for us. The light in the house at night always was shadowy and could become scary, for all we had were candles.

When they told us stories about Heshestawea, Red Woman, we got so scared that we wouldn't even go outside to the outhouse unless Grandma went with us.

Older people believed that the time to tell these mystery stories was in the wintertime. Older men visiting my father would tell stories about Old Man Coyote and Red Woman after they had smoked and prayed. I liked stories about women, and this one I remember about Red Woman.

The people were camping at a new camp. This woman had a little boy about four years old. He was playing outside and didn't come back in the tipi. His mother could not find him anywhere, so she went out into the hills and cried and prayed. In that way of fasting and crying she thought that she could get her boy back. Many years passed, and the boy was old enough to hunt and bring in deer. His mother still kept crying, hoping that her fasting and crying would lead a bird or some spirit person to help her, showing her with a vision what would happen. Finally the spirits told her that Red Woman had taken her son and that she would have a hard time getting him back, but they would help her.

Now, I must tell you that when people killed a buffalo, they used to take out the manyplies (third stomach) and another part full of holes. There are many layers to the manyplies, and when the Crow saw the pages of the Bible, they named it after the manyplies. The spirit told the woman that Red Woman used the Bible or manyplies for her comb and the perforated part for her perfume. There were three important things that belonged to Red Woman: her comb, perfume, and red paint. The spirit person instructed the woman to get these three things and then get her boy and start running. Red Woman would be in a deep sleep, but once awakened, she would start after them. In a final word, the spirit warned the mother, "Be sure and take along Red Woman's stick for digging roots." That made four things in the Crow way.

The mother came to where Red Woman held her boy and told him what he was to do. She got him to understand even though she could not get close to him. When Red Woman came home, she knew that the boy had talked with his mother. Red Woman said to herself, "I've got him nice and fat, and I'll eat him." When Red Woman told the boy that he had been talking with his mother, he tricked her with a question: "Why do you always say that I've seen my mother when you know that I've got you as a mother?" Then he went out and hunted for Red Woman and brought meat to her.

During the day Red Woman traveled a lot and became very tired. After eating she fell into a deep sleep. While Red Woman was fast asleep, the boy took the comb, perfume, red paint, and digging stick. He joined his mother, and they started running. They were frightened and did not look back because Red Woman made such a frightful appearance with her bushy hair. After running a long way, they did take a quick look back, and sure enough, Red Woman was coming after them. The boy was scared, but the spirits told him, "When she is about to get you, throw that Bible back, and that will delay her." When the mother threw the Bible back, it made layers of rocks, and Red Woman couldn't get over the rocks quickly as she had to climb one layer at a time. When she got to the top, the boy and his mother were out of sight. As Red Woman gained on them, the boy cried out, "Oh, mother, she's coming!" When Red Woman was about to get them, the mother threw down the part full of holes. Again a lot of rocks sprang up and Red woman had to climb up and down. She spent a whole day on the rocks, and the boy and his mother ran a long way. When Red Woman again was about to reach out and get them, the mother threw down a comb she herself had carved of porcupine skin. Trees sprang up like a thicket, and Red woman had a hard time getting through the trees. After that they spread Red Woman's perfume, and they heard her exclaim in anger, "Oh, they've got my perfume!" By the time Red Woman picked up all her perfume, the boy and his mother were coming to a big river. The boy knew that Red Woman was no swimmer. When Red Woman was about to catch them, they scattered the red paint, and she really became mad, as the paint was in small pieces.

While Red Woman was picking up her red paint, the boy and his mother walked to the other side of the river on Red Woman's digging stick. When Red woman came to the river, she tried to talk the mother into sharing the boy. "If you get me across, you and I will both claim this boy, and we'll both have him hunt for us; so put your stick across." The boy put the stick across and told Red Woman to climb onto it; when she was about halfway, he turned the stick, and Red Woman fell in the water and drowned. That is how this woman got her son back. She and her boy were able to do all this because a spirit was with them all the time, and the spirit helped them because the mother had gone out to fast and to cry for help.

You can see why we kids were afraid of Red Woman and the dark. We also were afraid of owls, and I'm still scared of owls. When an owl comes and hoots twice, you will have bad luck. That happened to me and Donnie, my second husband. He had a little girl by his first wife. The girl was sick when this owl came and hung around our house. I didn't like that, for every evening he would hoot twice, and one evening the owl even sat on our roof. That is a real bad sign. I told Donnie to scare it away. Then he hooted twice and flew away. The little girl died soon after. You know, owls change themselves into a person or a baby crying, or a dog barking, and they imitate you. Sometimes they break twigs and throw them at you. That's what happened to Donnie. This owl flew alongside him and threw a big twig at him. I remember, too, that an owl hooted just before my dad passed away. That's why I am scared of owls and believe that they are bad luck. Owls are ghosts who didn't join the Other Side People and who hang around places where people are buried.

Listening, Watching, and Learning

As a child I never did learn much from my mother. She was too busy tanning hides, making clothes, doing household chores, and helping with the haying to find time to teach me. She did everything herself, and I never even had to do dishes. My sister used to get mad and blurt out, "Make her work! You spoil her too much. She's lazy!" In time Mother did teach me how to sew and to bead, and I picked up quite a few things myself. I always said it was a wonder that I learned how to cook, sew, and bead, because Mother never let me do it. I did learn a lot about cooking by watching Mother and Robbie's wife. Mother baked bread and pies quite a lot, and she dried berries and meat. I guess it's just in me, for I turned out to be a pretty hard worker like my mother.

Mother was a skilled tanner. She tanned horsehides for rugs and cowhides to cover wagons. Cowhides were good wagon covers because they didn't let the wind get through. Buffalo hides were hard to tan, but mother tanned buffalo hides for all her children. These buffalo came from our tribal herd. I still have my buffalo hide. When the men in our family shot deer and elk, she would tan these hides, too. Mother also tanned and beaded buckskin dresses for all her grandchildren, all ten of them. When it was too cold to tan, she would sew, bead, and make quilts. She cut her own blocks for the quilts, put them together, and then gave the quilt to a grandchild.

In the Crow way it is not just your mother and father who teach you, but also grandmothers and grandfathers, and women of your own clan who are "mothers" to you. Older girls always had the task of watching younger ones. I can hear my parents yet tell my older sister, *"De weasak easa,"* — You, who are older, watch them."

I learned more from my mother's sister than from my own mother. I called my mother's sister (Mary Takes The Gun) *"masaka,"* just like my real mother. She taught us girls to be young ladies and cautioned us against shaming our brothers. "Don't make your brothers ashamed of you," she would say. She really made us respect our brothers and told us that we should not play with them after we became young ladies, around eight years of age. We were not to get so close to our brothers that we might touch them.

My mother and my female relatives never taught me anything about the blood coming. I was about twelve when I had my first period, and I was ashamed to tell my mother. Amy found out and told her. It wasn't the Crow way to talk about any sexual development until it happened. That was the way for boys, too. When I started to cry, Mother gave me some cloth and told me to use it. She also warned me to be careful because I could get pregnant. My father also talked to me at that time. He said,

"As much as I love you, if you ever get pregnant before you are married, you might just as well pack up your things and leave."

My sister was pretty smart. Amy noticed that Barney Old Coyote, our brother-in-law, wore one of those athletic supporters. She figured that this could be good for girls when they had their period. She made a pattern and then made one on the sewing machine. She used a piece of soft cloth or cheesecloth for absorbing. It worked so well that she could run around and play instead of staying at home in a room. She showed it to her friends and they all made one, but she never showed me how to make a belt. Amy didn't live with us, and I was never close to her. I learned about such things from the kids at school.

My parents were really strict about playing with our brothers. Also, you were not supposed to show off with your boyfriend, or smoke, or drink. But to have an illegitimate child was one of the worst things a girl could do, and it must have been a terrible thing to have happen in those days. I listened to my father, and what he told me stays with me to this day. I teach my grandchildren the same things, but today brothers sometimes quarrel with sisters, and pretty near all girls have a baby before they are married. It doesn't seem to make much difference now. I think the old days were best because children listened to and learned from the old people and had respect for them. Today, children have no respect for anyone.

As punishment, Mother spanked me, but Father never did. He was very gentle, and he would explain what we should do and tell us why. We all turned out pretty good. My mother was not warm and loving like my father. My brother Tom is like him, easygoing and calm. Mother yelled and scolded. I guess that's why I still remember the things my father told me.

Crows in the old days did not switch their children, but they did pour water up the noses of children who would not listen. Sometimes they rolled children up in buffalo robes. In my time they wrapped children in blankets or put them in a gunnysack and tied it, and sometimes they hung it up in a tree. Donnie and I did this to a daughter of my sister's son about thirty years ago.

Kids learned a lot just through listening, watching, and then doing. Our folks didn't lecture us much. They'd tell stories, especially on the long winter nights. That's when we listened and learned what to fear, what to do, and what to respect. We learned that Old Man Coyote, Esakuateh, along with his little companion, Shedapay, shaped the world, making all the rivers, lakes, and mountains. He also put the stars in their places and made all the different birds and animals.

The old people also told us that Old Man Coyote created people. Long ago he lived among the Crow and taught them to make bows and to chip stone arrow-heads. He also taught our people how to dream in a spirit way so they would come to know the medicine ways. It was Old Man Coyote who gave us our Indian ways—how to live as Crows; how to dream, to hunt, to make tipis; and how to get medicine to live by. The old people told us about this.

But Old Man Coyote was also a tricky person, and at times he could be real bad. On one visit to the Crow he tricked his way into marrying his own daughter, but he was found out and had to run out of camp just like a dog. Another time he tricked his mother-in-law into going on the warpath. At night in the brush war lodge made in the form of a tipi, he got an owl to hoot and to scare his mother-in-law into coming close to him; that way he had his way with her. A son-in-law isn't even supposed to look at his mother-in-law, and he isn't supposed to talk to her. He must talk to her through another person, or in the third person. My husband, Donnie, never spoke to my mother during the thirty-seven years she lived with us. He never sat down to eat at the same table with her until the last few years. They would not enter a building through the same door if they could help it. Now you can see how bad that Old Man Coyote was.

These winter stories taught us about the mysterious in life. This happened to a woman who was sitting with her friend under a tall ash tree, sewing. She looked up and saw a porcupine and thought she would get it to eat and use the quills for decoration. The porcupine kept climbing, and climbing, until the woman was so high the sky closed after her. She found herself before a tipi among the spirit persons. A young man approached her, and she had a son by him. He was the Sun, and because she did not stay away from the hole in the sky as he ordered, she lost her life. She wanted to go back to her people on earth, so she removed buffalo chips covering the hole in the sky and, taking her boy, started down a sinew rope. But the rope didn't quite reach the ground, and while she was dangling there, the spirits threw down a rock that killed her. The spirits saved the boy, and he became a hero, killing monsters who were eating people and other living things.

Crows always believed that the mysterious was important in their lives. They fasted and cried so that a spirit person would adopt them and bring them good luck. But you had to follow their rules, or you came to harm just like that woman.

Crow parents never pushed kids into learning but

waited for their interest to develop. Then a grandfather or older brother would show the boy how to shoot with a bow and arrow. Grandmothers and mothers showed girls how to make pan-fried bread, how to tan hides, and how to bead. When kids did something great, like shooting a deer for the first time, or nowadays, shooting the winning basket in a game, this was the time for parents, and especially the mother's relatives, to hold a giveaway. At this giveaway they honored the boy and thanked clan uncles and aunts with presents for the dream-blessings that made the boy's success possible.

Relatives were also our childhood teachers. Through their visits we got to understand who was a "brother" or a "sister" or a "mother." When my father's sister came to visit, my father would say, "There comes my sister. She is just like your mother." My favorite other "mother" was Scratches Face, Father's real sister. She was a pretty married lady, but she also made a name for herself with her giveaways. When my mother's sister came to visit, they told me, "She's your other mother." The first time I met my mother's brother was in Wyola at the mission church and school. He came on horseback and stayed overnight. They said, "Here's your older brother, *de sawday.*" He held me up, reached in his pocket, and gave me a silver dollar. I liked him, and that was the first dollar I ever got.

Visiting Relatives

When we went to visit relatives, it was a big thing, because we traveled with horses and wagons over nothing but wagon paths. My mother's relatives lived by Big Horn, or St. Xavier, as the community was called. We didn't see any of them very often, and when we went visiting, we usually stayed a month at a time. That way my "brothers" and "sisters" and I came to feel real close to each other, and that is true to this very day.

Mother's younger sister, Mary Takes The Gun, had the Indian name of Young Yellow Woman, or Beagatsheda in Crow. She lived on the other side of the Big Horn River. I always called her "Other Mother," and her children were like brothers and sisters, although they would be cousins in the White way. My parents usually made a trip in the spring while the snow was still melting, and we went again in the fall. The back of the wagon was loaded up. When we were all in the buggy, father would name each of us and tell us that the sun was shining over St. Xavier and that we all were going to have a good time. His saying this was like a wish-blessing, and we always did have fun at Other Mother's place.

We cut across the hills, following the wagon trails, and every little coulee would be filled with water high enough to reach the floor of the buggy. I'll never forget those trips! It took all day to get to the Big Horn River, and when it got dark we stayed with friends on this side of the river. The next morning, Other Mother's sons-in-law, Barney Old Coyote and Al Childs, came to get us when we shouted. They rode up and tied ropes to the buggy and wagon and pulled them across. Other Mother came, too, and took us across in her boat. I was only eight years old on one of these trips, and I was scared that the boat would turn over and I would be drowned. But Other Mother was not afraid of anything.

Our relatives always were happy to see us. They would ask, *"De shodaje?"* which means, "You, how are you?" Then they would add, "It's good to see you," *"De awaganichik."* Then when we left, they would always say, "Come again!" for Crows never like to say goodbye. In

Sisters Lizzie (Agnes's mother, seated) and Mary (Agnes's "other mother"), at Fort Custer, 1887. Courtesy Hardin Photo Service.

the old days it was important to ask where people had come from and where they were going; "Where do you come from?" and "Where are you going?" are traditional greetings even today.

Once we got to the other side of the river we all rode horses to the house. Our relatives wouldn't let us do anything, and following Crow custom, they fed us right away.

Other Mother and her husband were better off than my folks. My sister, Amy, used to live with them for weeks at a time. They had lots of cattle, and one time they branded over six hundred calves. Takes The Gun would lasso the calves, and Other Mother would castrate them, working along just like the men. They always ate what they took out in the castration. It was like a little sausage. When Takes The Gun got too old and couldn't work so hard, they sold off the cattle. Neither one of their sons-in-law wanted to work with cattle.

On our visits they always killed a beef for us. Other Mother's husband would say to her, "Don't take any of the beef. I'm giving it to them. If they want to give you some, they can do it." Mother and Father would cut the meat into strips and dry it. It took about three to four days to dry the meat. When this was done, my two mothers would pound the dried meat, and sometimes they mixed tallow and chokecherries with it to make pemmican. Mother took the dried meat and pemmican home, but she always cooked some of the beef and gave it to her younger sister.

Other Mother always had a big garden, and she canned vegetables. During our fall visit, when the plums were ripe, we'd get into the wagon and draw up right under the trees. It was easy to pick plums. They laid the plums, chokecherries, and berries on the long porch to dry, and we kids ate all we wanted. My two mothers also would dig Indian turnips and mash them before drying. When we returned home, we always had several flour and sugar sacks filled with dried fruits and turnips.

Every day Other Mother made lunch for us. She made trips to Hardin for supplies and bought everything by the case, fifty pounds of lard, and one hundred pounds of sugar. She bought little cubes of sugar and gave them out by the handfuls to us kids. She was a generous person and had a lot of friends. There were even some wandering Crees camping on their land, for these Crees had no reservation. The Crees helped out with the ranch chores in exchange for watering and grazing their horses. Other Mother used to take them groceries, and one time she got them to build a corral for our horses when we came for the Fourth of July celebration.

We kids always had a great time at Other Mother's place because we just played and played. Joy, Robbie's oldest daughter, always came along, and there was my "sister" Suzanne Old Coyote and my "brothers" Frank and George Takes The Gun. Every morning we girls made our plans for the day, but first, we had to go to a nearby spring and bring water bags for the house. Then we ran to play and put up our small tipis. At times Other Mother gave us real food to cook, and we even made berry pudding. We had fun swimming in the river, and I can remember how George and my brother Tom made a little sweat lodge and played at sweating. Sometimes we'd go into the hills and just play around while we walked. We were always back before dark, because we were scared of that Red Woman.

Other Mother's place had lots of barns and shacks to hide behind, and playing hide-and-seek was great fun.

We also played tag and pom-pom-pullaway. In the evenings before dark we played old bear, which was our favorite. We'd make a line and swing back and forth to avoid the bear who tried to grab and bite someone. If you were the last in line you usually got bit, and then you were the bear.

CHAPTER 5

School, Education, and Church

Mission and Public School

I didn't have too much to say about my education, and I never thought much about what I wanted to do with an education. But the law said that Indian children had to go to school just like the White kids. I remember that I wanted to get a good education, and if it had been my way, I'd have completed high school.

My schooling never went beyond the seventh grade. Four of these grades were in the Baptist mission school, and three were in public school in Lodge Grass. Then I spent a few months in Oregon at Chemawa. My brother Robbie's boy Buford passed away, and when Robbie came to take his daughter Winona home for the funeral, my folks wanted me to come home, too. After the funeral, they wouldn't let me return to Chemawa because they wanted me to get married. None of us went far in school in those days. People really didn't know what to do with an education, and they didn't see any reason to go to school just to learn English.

My mother was the one who wanted me to stay home and get married. I still get mad every time I think about it, and I feel it was her fault I didn't get to go back to Chemawa. I didn't argue with her because of what the Bible said: "Honor thy father and thy mother."

Getting to school in those days was a real problem. When the weather was good, my brother Tom and I rode horseback for three miles on a horse trail, carrying our lunches in little bags hanging from our saddles. Being a boy, Tom didn't like to carry his lunch, so I carried it for him. School started at nine, and we got out at four o'clock. Then we all ran for our horses, and we raced them all the way home.

When we got home, Father would be waiting for us by the barn, and he would unsaddle the horses and give them water and oats. He put them in the barn to get them ready for the next day, for our horses stood all day outside the schoolhouse without food and water. It was tough on horses in those days because we ran them hard. I got to be a pretty good rider, like a boy. I could ride and jump over ditches, and that was fun.

My brother Tom was really good to me and looked after me. He wasn't rough but was nice and got along well with everybody. I don't remember that he ever mistreated me since we were young. Before it was time for me to start school, he tried to teach me the one, two, threes of arithmetic, how to count, and my ABCs. He told me that if I learned them, school wouldn't be so hard. Even though I learned it, I never did get good at arithmetic.

I didn't start school until I was seven years old. I was so sick the year before that I nearly died and stayed weak for a long time. I went to the Baptist mission school built by the Crow close to Dr. Petzoldt's log cabin house. Mrs. Petzoldt was my first teacher, and she was very good. None of us liked our next teacher, Miss Wafford. She was mean and cranky and didn't like Indian kids the way Miss Shaw, who came later, did. Miss Wafford punished me several times, hitting my hands with a ruler. One

Agnes and her Baptist mission schoolmates, around 1920. Front row, left to right: Joe Carpenter, Martin Spotted Horse, Gerald Red Wolf, Genevieve White Arm, Joe Medicine Crow, Albert Bad Bear, and Jimmy Passes. Second row, left to right: Thomas Bad Bear, Leo Not Afraid, Matilda Deputy, and Gary Bad Bear. Third row, left to right: Alexander Hill, Jim Medicine Tail, Kelly Passes, Rena Lefthand, Agnes Yellowtail, and Mary Ann Carpenter. Courtesy Hardin Photo Service.

time she put me in a closet for half an hour. But later Miss Wafford and I got to be friends. She wrote me from St. Louis, and Donnie and I visited her one time when returning from a meeting back East. Her place was cold and uncomfortable in the big brick apartment house where she lived. It made me feel bad to see her so old in this way. She passed away two years later.

We were all in one room at the mission school, and there were no White kids, just some breeds like Chatham and Howe, who didn't speak Indian. There were about forty of us—two rows of boys and two of girls—and one teacher taught all the classes. Then there were ten or twelve first graders, who had their own special table.

We started class with a prayer given by the teacher with everyone bowing his head. Then we had to sing for our teacher, "Good morning to you, good morning, dear teacher, we're glad to see you!" To first graders all this English was strange and hard because we only knew Crow and spoke our own language at home and at play. Even by fourth grade, our English wasn't real good.

They taught us arithmetic, reading, spelling, history, and geography. History was mostly about religion. The teacher told us how in the Holy Land they got down on their knees to pray, like the Arabs do. She taught us what each state grew in the way of corn, beans, and potatoes. I didn't really like any of the subjects, except history and geography some. I was pretty good at spelling. We had a good basketball team of Indian girls, and we played against White girls. I liked that.

During recess our teacher didn't organize our games, so we played Annie-over, skipped rope, and watched the boys play marbles or knife-in-the-ground-hits (mumble-ty-peg). Because brothers and sisters were expected to show respect by not roughhousing or touching each other, the girls stuck pretty much together and so did the boys.

At lunchtime friends used to share good things, but the younger ones had to be careful of the older girls. They were mean to us and would take our lunches and eat all the good stuff.

My first public school in Lodge Grass was a two-room frame building located down in the river bottom. They used it as a community hall, too. I must have been eleven when I went there. Then they built the school up on the bluff above Lodge Grass, where the elementary and high schools now are. They sent the bigger kids up there. I was in the sixth grade, and I remember Miss Ruth, Miss Holliday, and Miss Hamilton because they all liked Indian kids. Miss Hamilton especially liked my brother Tom and Pete Lefthand. Already Tom and Pete were close friends and partners. Most Crow boys make friends when they are young and hold on to them for life. They went everywhere together and danced as partners during the war dance. They shared whatever they had.

The Indians stayed pretty much together and didn't go around with White kids. There were more Whites than Indians in the public school, while at the mission school we were all Indians. We weren't used to White kids, and they weren't used to us. White boys would say things to Indian boys and taunt them, and then there would be a fight. I know of some Indian boys who just quit school because it was so hard to get along with the White kids. I had a White girlfriend whose parents owned a drugstore in town. She used to take me there and treat me to ice cream and pop, and they gave me everything I liked. But then they sold the drugstore and moved away.

At school they made us play basketball on a team mixed with Whites. At first it wasn't too good, but every year we got better acquainted. I got along pretty well with the White girls and even had some friends.

I was about sixteen when they sent me away to Chemawa in Oregon. A whole bunch of us went. There were my "daughters" — Joy, Winona, and Marjery, my brother Robbie's girls. My "brother" Frank Takes The Gun also went along. He was my mother's sister's son. The others who went were Tilly Walking Bear, Matilda Deputy, Louis Walks On The Ice, and John Half. Pete Lefthand's sister, Rena, also was with us, as well as Kelly Passes, Jack Littlenest, Elizabeth Fitzpatrick, and Edith and Dora Blackhawk.

The summer before we left, the wife of the man who gave out lease money came from Crow Agency and taught Indian women how to cook and make pies. She also taught sewing to us girls. Each of us brought our own material, and she helped us cut it out and showed us how to make dresses. When we went off to Chemawa, we all had new dresses. I was proud that I had made my own.

I liked Chemawa very much, and we all owed it to a Mrs. Cope who talked to our parents and told them that it would be good for us. Chemawa was so pretty, with the pine trees and flowers, and there were lots of kids and many friends. I was never lonesome. We met Eskimos, Flatheads, and some Indians from California. I just loved Chemawa, but I only got to stay there for about three months.

There was one Indian teacher at Chemawa during my stay. They didn't teach anything special, mostly English and reading. They taught girls how to sew and to wash, and boys took courses in blacksmithing and carpentry. That was what we learned at government schools. We also had to go to church, whether Protestant or Catholic, according to our church.

We had to march to breakfast, and as we passed by a big walnut tree, we used to pick and eat walnuts. The food wasn't bad, but we got gravy almost every meal. That's why today we call gravy at our meals "government gravy." We got it three times a day.

Orchards and berry farms were nearby, and we used to sneak a few apples and peaches. The school took us to pick loganberries, and we always had fun doing that. They gave us a shoe box to put them in. What we liked to do most was to go to Salem on the trolley. If we had any per capita coming, they would keep it for us in the office. Then on a weekend we would pick it up and head for Salem to shop.

Donnie and I had a chance to go to Chemawa again in 1962 when Milton Yellow Mule wanted us to drive him to see the "Big Water" before he died. When Milton saw the big water (ocean), he couldn't get over it. He walked on the shore and picked up shells, and whenever a big wave came, he'd run from it as fast as he could.

At Chemawa we visited with our old missionary teachers from the Crow Baptist mission, Miss Olds and Miss Johnson. They were up for retirement. Chemawa had changed, and there was a big highway running by the school. I hardly recognized the place.

Education and Travel

English was the big task for us and also for the teachers when I was growing up. The teachers couldn't always make us understand what they wanted, so they looked for a Crow boy or girl who knew some English or could pick it up easily. Teachers had to have interpreters just as the missionaries and the government agents did. The Crow needed interpreters, too, to find out what to do when they made a lease for their lands. Lulu White Bear, a White teacher who married Russell White Bear, took quite an interest in my second husband, Donnie, when he was going to school at Reno. She taught him English, and sometimes he lived with them because she wanted him to learn the language. He was the one the teachers always chose to interpret for the Whites. Lulu probably picked him because he wasn't bashful like the others and wasn't afraid to speak up in class.

Even in the thirties and forties Crow children entered school without any real background in English. They didn't have interpreters in the classroom then, and inter-preters were no longer used in churches either. By the time the Indians were in fourth grade in public school, most of them were too far behind to keep up with the White kids in reading. Because of this, they became more and more bashful when called on to recite, espe-cially if they had *ewatkusua,* or joking relatives, in class who would tease them later if they made a mistake.

Boys liked hunting and horseback riding, and at home the grandfathers filled them with stories of the old hunting and fighting days. During the summer in the shade of cottonwood trees near the church in Lodge Grass, White Arm and other old men often gathered and drew a crowd of boys and young men to hear their stories. They had many jokes to tell about foolish peo-ple, as well as stories about exciting escapes and horse raids.

In class, boys and girls retreated behind the safety of their reading books and often drew pictures of camping, horses, deer, buffalo, and tipis. They knew they were different from White kids, who could beat them at reading, spelling, and arithmetic. Books were a part of the White nature, but Indian kids learned from the old people and from the medicine fathers.

Besides, there wasn't much chance to study in a one- or two-room log cabin crowded with several kids, a mother and father, and probably a brother or sister of the mother or father. Usually there was a lot going on at the house in the evening, and we had only candlelight, kerosene, or Coleman lanterns to study by until we got rural electrification in the thirties under Roosevelt.

Basketball was one thing about school that we all liked. I think that is why a lot of Crow boys kept going until high school. In the Eshebea camp, you could see young kids throwing baskets through barrel hoops all the time. All this practice helped Crows to develop a kind of team play with partners, and they usually made up most of the team at the grade and high schools.

I don't know why Crows took to basketball so much. In our games we always look for individual winners. Men shot arrows at a target, and the winner could pick up the arrows of the losers. Or men would compete by throwing a long arrow at a rolling hoop. It's that way in basketball, too, even though you are a member of a team. You can still be the best scorer, or the one who wins the game with a final basket. Then you will be honored with a giveway in which you give presents to your clan uncles and aunts, and they sing praise songs for you. To be an outstanding player, you need to get a medicine from a clan uncle and treat it with respect. There was this high school player who carried a medicine feather to help him make baskets. He was really good. Then he began to miss, and he turned against the medicine and threw it down a toilet. Later on he shot himself.

My generation was lucky to get through grade school before dropping out and getting married. People expected you to get married, and there wasn't much else to look forward to. People weren't ready to try to get a job away from the reservation, and few had the education or training to take a job in a city. It was hard to be away from your folks and friends and go to a strange place where people didn't know you. That was why Ataloa didn't want to go away to Denver to live with a White family.

Before the war, Crows didn't travel much outside the reservation, and so they didn't know much about the world beyond Billings or Sheridan. Some had been to Oklahoma for Peyote worship, and there were delegates for the tribe who were sent off to Washington. The automobile got some of our young people interested in auto mechanics. Before we were married, Donnie went away to Kansas City, Missouri, to the Coleman Electrical School and learned about electrical wiring and auto mechanics. For a while he worked in garages at Crow Agency and in Lodge Grass. He was always studying, trying to learn new skills, such as carpentry and plumbing. He used that knowledge to fix up our house.

I think the war really started to change us, for many of our young men were sent to Europe and to the Pacific. Some of us who stayed at home traveled to Toppenish, Washington, where we worked in the orchards. It was there that we first saw Iron Hat prisoners. Some of our veterans told us when they came back that we needed to take charge of our own lands instead of letting Whites make all the money. About that same time, more of our people began to speak out for education. Donnie always thought that the Crow parents had the responsibility to see to it that their children got a good education. Donnie said if Indians were going to become independent in an economic way they needed to have control of their own lands. They had to be free to make their own decisions, even if they made mistakes. He meant that Crows should not lease their small pieces of land to Whites individually but instead should pool their lands and lease them to Indians organized in livestock associations, like the Lodge Grass livestock association Donnie helped form. When Crows got a little hard up or were planning to have a giveaway they sold their lands to Whites. Already over forty percent of the best lands located in the valleys close to water were owned by non-Indians, and Donnie tried to stop this. But to make a living off the land, Crows would have to work and live like White people. That was the price they had to pay for the refrigerators, electric stoves, clothes, radios, televisions, and cars that were becoming very important to them.

Education seemed to be the big thing behind all this, and they realized you needed an education to pick up the skills to get a job and help you stay on the job like the Whites. Education would show you how to manage your lease money. Crows were beginning to realize they needed training in business if they wanted to develop the game, timber, mineral, and recreational resources of the tribe so they would provide jobs for their own people.

Donnie always wanted to free Indians from the "competency" regulations of the government, for the regulations kept Indians from taking care of their own affairs. He never did like that word, *competency,* but he knew that a person must know how to manage property if he was to succeed. To get out from under the government regulations, Donnie sponsored a resolution to establish a standard test for competency for Crow Indians that they could administer themselves. Just as he feared, the tribal council made it so easy that anyone who ever applied could be judged competent. Then they amended the resolution so that the children of "competents" automatically became "competent," too. That easy determination of competence led many Crows to make five-year leases with White ranchers and to draw the entire five-year lease money in advance. The way it worked out, the ranchers held back one year of interest, and quite a few Crows got only four years of lease money or less. When that happened, the council worked up a resolution that allowed Crow lessors to break their five-year leases, but they had to pay back money advanced for the years left in the contract. Leases were seldom broken, and this arrangement was not popular with the Whites, who intimidated the Indians with threats of court action.

The other big problem Crow farmers and ranchers faced had to do with the many heirs owning a piece of land. Donnie and some others formed the Little Horn Livestock Association to get into the cattle business. They did get some leases from Crow landowners, but it wasn't long before the owners asked for an advance on the lease money. Donnie and the other association members didn't have money for these constant advances, so they were forced to disband their livestock association. Somehow these small pieces of land with their many heirs had to be united so Crows who wanted to farm or to run cattle could purchase them. But how to do it? Donnie thought that the tribe could purchase the land and then work out a long-term lease plan for the Crow buyers. The idea was to get Crows to buy into their reservation lands rather than leasing or selling land to non-Indians. But most Crow landowners preferred to lease to White ranchers because they got cash at the signing of the contract and, if they became hard up, they could get cash advances. Crow Indian ranchers didn't have the ready cash for advances, and the landowners couldn't wait until the cattle were sold to get their lease money for the year.

I was lucky with the land where I now live. Thirteen people had a share in this land of eighty acres, and Gabriel Moccasin had the biggest share. Gabriel was the son of a brother of my father, and so he was a "brother" to me. I wanted to buy his share, but he said, "I'll give it to you." He had a lot of land through inheritance. My mother gave me her share, and so did all my other brothers and sisters. My own land by allotment was way out toward the Wolf Mountains, and my husband's allotted lands were by the Big Horn Mountains, miles apart. We wanted a place in the valley, so we could farm and have cattle.

My son, Bobby, wanted his boys to be good athletes because he himself was quite a basketball player. He even named his boys after outstanding players. He did not want his boys to have much do with the "night kids" in Lodge Grass, who stay out till all hours drinking and hanging around street corners. He wanted his children to learn to work. All his children have a good education. Arnold taught at Busby among the Northern Cheyennes, but now he raises cattle. Leonard is teaching at the Lodge Grass High School. Bedene works for Head Start, and Ada has a job in Lodge Grass. Duane had two years of college. My adopted daughter, Ferale, is the secretary of the hospital at Crow Agency, and her husband, Bill, works for the Bureau of Indian Affairs there. Ataloa, who was adopted by my mother, is a nurse and is married to a Northern Cheyenne. Donnie and I kept after Ferale and Ataloa in their studies, and they did well in school. The one I worry about is Duane, for he took up surveying and doesn't have a job. He did have an offer of a survey job away from here, but he didn't take it because he didn't want to leave his family and friends.

Indian Worship and Adoption

My mother and father grew up in the Indian way of worshipping. They fasted and belonged to the Tobacco Society, as did many Crows in their day. The Tobacco Society had quite a few separate groups in it, and my parents were members of the Duck Society. I still have some of those little duck wings my mother gave me.

A person became a member of the Tobacco Society by adoption. I was adopted by Packs The Hat and his wife when I was twelve. I miss them, as they were really good to me. Mrs. Packs The Hat was the sister of the mother of my brother-in-law, John Whiteman. The Packs The Hats first asked my parents if they could adopt me, and when my parents agreed, they set a time in the spring. They took me into the adoption lodge and sang medicine songs for me three times, and the fourth time they adopted me. I didn't have anything to do except sit and let them sing and pray for me. They fixed a lunch for me each time they sang, with oranges and bananas, which were special at that time.

At the adoption, four couples (a man and his wife) sang for me, and each couple gave me a medicine song. After they sang it four times it became my song. When Packs The Hat sang his special song, all the other couples joined in, and then they made me get up and dance along with my adopted father and mother, the Packs The Hats. Then I was adopted. I selected four medicines that the couples had out on display because that was part of the adoption.

During my adoption they also passed the Duck medicine bag around, sending it clockwise in the direction of
the sun. Each person held it in front of him, after
smoking it in the cedar incense, and made a wish. Next
they passed the rattle, and each person made a half-
circle with it to the left. There was always a special man
who lit the pipe for prayer. He gave the pipe to an outstanding man and then to the men singers for prayer. The
pipe lighter sang two or three songs, and then the women
got up and danced. Women don't sing much in the adoptions in most Crow ceremonies. Sometimes if you went to
the adoption ceremony, you had to sing your medicine
song and dance. If a woman was in there by herself,
sometimes her adoptive parents sang for her. The singing
often took all night. When they were through with the
adoption singing, they put out fried bread, chokecherry
pudding, and soup. They didn't have much, and only
certain women had the right to pass the food. After
eating, people visited a little and went home.

At my adoption, father and mother piled presents for
the Packs The Hats behind them and also draped Pendleton blankets over their shoulders. My Tobacco parents in turn fixed me up with a buckskin dress, beaded
leggings, a shawl, and a horse to ride. They also gave me
several elk-tooth dresses, but the teeth were made of
bone. That's what I got, but nowadays the children being
adopted get automobiles, horses, cows, hundreds of
blankets, a tipi, and dishes. You need to be rich like a
millionaire now to get adopted, but people still do it.

In my childhood you were adopted only in the spring.
Now Tobacco Society members adopt any time, even
though the older people say it is not right. They adopt all
during the summer, but they meet only at night for their
adoption medicine songs.

Adoptions should take place right after members of
the Tobacco Society plant the tobacco. Before planting,
the tobacco must be mixed with certain medicines to
make it grow. There used to be four men who had the
right to mix the tobacco, but since Chester Medicine
Crow and Matthew Good Luck passed away, there are
only two. The mixers put together their own sacred
medicines, and the only way you can learn it is to be
adopted by them and to buy the right.

To get ready for the planting the Tobacco Society first
puts up a large tipi. Inside the tipi they make little altars
on the ground, and they hold medicine sings and dances
for the tobacco. Then a woman with a good reputation,
and who has a Tobacco medicine bundle, leads a procession to the planting ground. They sing a special song
four times on leaving the lodge. The woman leader
walks with her medicine bundle on her back and stops
four times along the way to sing. At the fourth stop,
young boys run with medicine bundles of the different
societies and try to reach the garden first. To get there
first means good luck for everyone connected with that
bundle.

At the garden, the members take their tobacco seeds
to the mixers and in return are given a blessed pemmican ball. If you give to all four mixers, you get four
pemmicans. By this time people are ready to eat and to
rest, for they have been cutting poles and brush for the
fence. The men built a fence around the garden. The
families, using sticks painted by men or women who
have the right, dig small holes and put just a little of the
mixed seeds in. These digging sticks also have eagle
feathers attached. Before leaving the planting, they always make sure the garden has a good fence.

I was too young at my adoption to take part in the

planting, but I did make my sticks for the fence and got my pemmican. After a moon passed, the heads of the societies returned to the garden to see how the tobacco was growing. They left the tobacco until the berries showed, then they picked it and kept it for the next year. My adopted daughter's Indian name has to do with the growing of that tobacco: Ferale is known as Goes To See Her Garden.

Joining the Mission Church

My father and mother gave up that medicine bundle worship after they learned about God in the Christian way, but they both continued to go to the Tobacco adoptions and plantings. While father was in the Tobacco Society, he belonged to the Catholic church until he changed to the Baptist church. That's the way it was with mother, too. She went to the Tobacco while she was a Baptist, and she didn't stop going until a few years before she passed away. Mother was a strong member of the Baptist church all her life. She prayed a lot and went to church every Sunday.

Father changed from the Catholic to the Baptist church because Father Rabaud hurt his feelings. Up Lodge Grass Creek there was a little Catholic church called St. Ann, and Father Rabaud went there once a month to say mass. When it was time, father would say, "We're going to church because Father Rabaud is going to be there." So we would go over the hills with the team and buggy, staying overnight at my father's brother's place, at Moccasin Top's. Father confessed to the Catholic priest at that time. But when my brother and I started to school, Father Rabaud asked my father if he would send us kids to the school at St. Ann. Father told him this was not possible. He said, "My house is in the Little Horn Valley, and it is too far to send the kids to St. Ann's." Then Father Rabaud told my father that if he didn't send us to St. Ann's mission school, Father Rabaud would no longer hear his confession. That hurt my father's feelings, and he said he would not go to the Catholic church anymore. I remember his saying to my mother, "I'll start going to your church, the Baptist church. That's where my kids and wife go, and I'll go there. That priest hurt my feelings." He started going to the Baptist church, and he never did go back to the Catholic church. He had his funeral in the Baptist church.

I liked the Tobacco Society and went to it even after I was a Baptist. Dr. Petzoldt baptized me a Baptist about the same time I was adopted into the Tobacco Society. After I married Donnie, I gave up the Tobacco worship because Donnie didn't want medicine bags between him and God. The way I look at it now, I don't believe in the old birds that they used in medicine. I don't think I'll ever go back to the Tobacco Society. Like Donnie, I don't want anything between me and my God. I know that Christ is a jealous God, and he doesn't want us to go back to that. My sister, Amy, and her husband are still pretty active in the Tobacco worship and are members of the Baptist church.

We Crows call the church the House of God, Adachewagawacheh. The church is where you pray to God. People pray in different ways and places. Some go to the sweat lodge to pray, some have the Tobacco ceremony or the Sun Dance, and others pray in the Peyote tipi. With me, ever since I was a girl of twelve, I just stayed with the Baptist church. I went to church every Sunday, and the church came first before I did anything else, like going on a picnic. My parents taught me about God, and they did give up the medicine bags. That is why I gave up the medicine bags and why the church means so much to me. I never could get up in front of people and pray until Miss Olds taught me how to pray out loud. Now I can pray in a crowd of people and not feel ashamed.

I guess I learned a lot about praying from my father because he was a good Christian man. He used to walk a little ways from the house and pray for all of us, and he always told us before going to sleep to thank God for the new day that was coming. I remember that when there was a new moon, my grandmother and father would say, "Come on out, children, let's pray." I can still hear my father as he raised me up: "Maybe you'll grow to be up this high, just a little way, the next day a little higher, the third day a little higher, and on the fourth day you'll grow big." Then they looked forward to the next new moon, praying, "If it's Thy will, then we will live to the next new moon." I don't know why they were so happy with the new moon. We don't do that anymore, and it seems like we're getting away from what our parents used to do. It's just a new moon to us now, and it doesn't mean anything. But after all, God created the moon, the stars, the sun, and the wind and water. When I thank Him for the Creation, I use the words of my parents when I pray.

We always have our children pray at the table so they can learn how. Right now we're teaching my grandchild, Leonard's little girl, how to pray. I am teaching her this prayer:

> God is great, God is good,
> And we thank You for our food,
> By His hand must thine be fed,
> Give us, Lord, our daily bread. Amen.

Jerry, who is three years old, is also learning it.

On Communion Sunday we prayed in Crow for all the people:

Akbatatdea	*ahoway*
Maker Of Everything	thank You
Akbatatdea	*ahoway*
Maker Of Everything	thank You
Checheduk	*ahoway*
Remember us	thank You
checheduk	*ahoway*
remember us	thank You
Awas aygyak	*ahoway*
Down look	thank You
awas aygyak	*ahoway*
down look	thank You
Baagukoriuk	*chewagaawagoway*
You up there	pray for me up there
ak-kay	
Father	
Ahoway	*ahoway*
Thank You	thank You

When people prayed for church members, they mentioned the sick and prayed that the younger generation would have a better education and life. They thanked God for home and family and for everything received from above—autos, clothing, food. I remember one woman praying, "Thank our Lord for the missionaries who are here to tell us of the Jesus Road." It was the missionaries who taught us to pray in the Christian way. Mrs. Petzoldt taught us little songs, and one I remember was "Jesus loves me, Praise Him, Praise Him." In Sunday School, I always taught the children what was in the Sunday School books, and I used Petzoldt's little songs and verses to teach the first, second, and third graders. I taught them to be sure to praise the Lord.

I learned how important praising the Lord is for your faith when my adopted grandson, Duane, came back from the army. He was drinking all the time. Donnie and I brought him up in the Baptist church, and I didn't understand why Duane turned out that way. So I began to praise the Lord, praising Him for what Duane was, and I came to accept Duane for what he was. From this I learned that you must praise the Lord for everything. If I don't have faith, I'll be crying. You just leave it up to Him. He knows best.

The old church that Dr. Petzoldt built in back of his place burned down, and he raised enough money to build the church we now have on land donated by White Arm. They used the schoolhouse for services until the new church was built. I was about twelve years old then, and I remember Dr. Petzoldt wouldn't baptize you until you could understand what the Church and Christian life meant.

On Sundays Father hitched up the horses, and we all drove to church in the buggy. Some of the families came a long way. We had church till noon, and everybody brought a lunch and ate it there. People looked forward to eating and visiting together. About two o'clock they had another service, stopping around four o'clock. The children were all up front, and we didn't run around and play in church the way kids do now. Sometimes during the week they had a box social and games. People came from Crow Agency by train and went back on the train about three in the morning. They called that the Thirty-One Train from its number.

We had a lot of members when Dr. Petzoldt and Miss Olds were here. Then other denominations came in, and a lot of our members left to become Catholics, Pentecostals, and even Peyote worshippers. We've lost quite a few to these churches. Nowadays children don't like to go to church. I had trouble with my family, too. Donnie and I used to take Duane to church every Sunday, but now that he is grown we can't make him go to church. Young people aren't interested in church work, and nowadays only a few go to the Sunday School classes.

In my own case I was lucky that my husband, Donnie, was a strong Baptist, and in that way nothing much changed in my life. We were always at the revivals, and I used to go with Donnie to meetings when they were close by. One time we went together as delegates to Green Lake, Wisconsin. We went with Miss Olds after Dr. Petzoldt retired. Donnie and I were always active in church work, especially with young people.

The Christian way of living is very important and means a lot to me. I leave it up to God. As a child I was very sick and was on a strict diet for two years. Through faith I was healed by that medicine man with his sucking pipe. When I had a gallbladder problem and had it removed through surgery, I was cured of that through faith. I love God and trust Him in everything.

I try to be a good person and try to talk to everybody. I think people trust me a lot, like those stores in Lodge Grass, because I always try to do the right thing, pay my bills, and live a good life. I read my Bible every night before I go to bed, because that way I feel close to the Lord.

CHAPTER 6

Courtship and Marriage

Boyfriends

When I was about fourteen, my parents kept a close watch on me and never let me stay out alone. That's the way it was for girls in my time, but we sometimes sneaked off to town or to meet our boyfriends. Boys could not come to the house to see us, so they would send a sister or another relative with a message telling where and when to meet. Sometimes a boyfriend would come to the house after dark and give a whistle for you to come out. I always looked for a chance to see my boyfriend at a dance or giveaway. When we met we never held hands but would say a few words and smile, and maybe make a secret date for another meeting. But you would not meet with boyfriends in front of your parents or brothers. We never met at the church because our parents were very strict and told us that church was not the place to visit with your boyfriend. Now the kids hold hands and copy the White kids.

Courting in secret was the old Crow way. A young man tried to meet a girl while she was alone, bringing water or working away from the tipi. The boys had a kind of wooden flute that they played as a signal, and when the girl heard it, she tried to find a way to meet him. Sometimes the poles with the flaps that controlled

the fire would get moved and smoke filled the tipi.
When the girl went out to fix them, there would be her
boyfriend.

Girls weren't supposed to have a baby before marriage
because that would shame their brothers. In the old days
when this happened to a girl, she tried jumping off a
rock or pressed hard against a post to make the baby
come out. When a girl got married, the boy's family paid
for her with horses; dressed her up with fine clothes,
moccasins, and quillwork; and gave her a tipi with all the
furnishings. But if a girl had a baby before she was
married, the boy's family wouldn't do much for her or
her relatives. Her father and brothers would not get
many horses. Marriages were arranged by parents or an
older brother, and if the girl didn't like the arrangement,
she had to run away to another camp with her boyfriend
to have things her way. That was a hard thing to do, but
some did it.

First Marriage

I met my boyfriend at a Fourth of July celebration when I
was fifteen. He wanted to marry me, but my folks
wouldn't let me, so he married someone else. My parents
picked out a husband for me and made me marry in the
old way.

It happened this way. My older brother Robbie took a
bunch of Crows to Washington, D.C., and I went along. I
was about fourteen. Willie Bends saw me and decided I
would make a good wife for his son, Warren. After we
came back, he talked to my folks and offered my brother
horses and my parents some money. I cried and carried
on because I had a boyfriend I liked, but I was afraid of
my folks. They told me I couldn't live with them any-

more, and they wouldn't claim me as their child. Then they said, "But if you do our will, and then if you are not happy, you can separate. Then later on you can marry anyone you want." I didn't know Warren, so his father brought him to our house for us to meet.

We were married on June twenty-fifth at Reno, when they were celebrating the Custer Battlefield Day. Warren's parents met us at the gate and told us our camp was ready. His mother and father put up a tipi for me and furnished it with Indian dresses, shawls, blankets, rugs, dishes, knives, forks, and spoons. My mother-in-law said, "*Beagata,* your tipi is ready for you." They took me to the tipi and said, "It's all yours."

Muskrat Woman, Warren's clan aunt, dressed me in an elk-tooth dress with beaded things, and people came and looked in the tipi to see what I had gotten. Then they put me on a horse, and Warren's clan uncle led me around the camp, telling people that these were all the things they had given me for wedding presents. Willie Bends and Warren followed behind. Willie sang a praise song and called out, "See what they are doing for her. This is Blackears [Warren's Indian name], and this is his wife, Sits Among The Cattails."

When I got off the horse, everything they had given became mine. It is our custom for the bride to pick out anything she wants. After that, she calls her "sisters" and tells them to take anything they want—elk-tooth dresses, blankets, mufflers—whatever they want. I picked out a buckskin dress and all the blankets and shawls I wanted. I gave the rest to my "sisters," who were married to my three brothers. My brothers, Robbie, Carson, and Tom, each gave a horse to their new brother-in-law, Warren Bends.

It was a sad wedding for me. Warren was terribly

bashful and didn't pay any attention to me. I don't think we spoke a word until it was all over. I was so unhappy and was crying inside all the time.

Warren's mother had a sister in Pryor. When the Crow had a big camp and celebration there in August, this sister put up another tipi with beaded goods, including Indian-type saddles. They made me parade again although we had already been married in June. I got a second tipi with good things in it. In return my own mother was supposed to give beaded moccasins, a buckskin shirt, a saddle horse, and a cowboy hat to Warren. My parents could wait about a year before they had to do this, but if his parents wanted them sooner for a celebration, my folks would have to get them together.

We stayed in the camp at Reno for three days until the camp broke up, and then Warren and I went to his parents' place to live. In buffalo-hunting days a young man took his bride to live in a tipi pitched near that of his parents. In our case we lived in the same house with them. It was a two-bedroom house with a kitchen and a living room. We had our own bedroom.

There were two young girls in my husband's family, one about two and the other about seven. Bertha, the seven-year-old, really liked me and kept telling her grandmother that she would take me as a sister. Today Bertha and I are good friends and get together once in a while for a talk. Donnie, my second husband, and I visited her sometimes to eat at her house because her husband, Hugh Little Owl, and Donnie were clan brothers.

After I was married, my mother instructed me to help with washing the dishes and to do whatever I could to help. I wasn't just to sit there. Crows never come right out and ask a new daughter-in-law to do anything. It is up to her if she wants to help. They usually don't tell a daughter-in-law to do anything whatever, and that was the way my mother-in-law was. After you have a chance to get used to your in-laws, that was when you washed the dishes and helped around the house.

Life with my in-laws was never happy. They were poor people, and some slept on the floor. I was used to eating with a knife, fork, and spoon, but they had only a few spoons. My mother-in-law would fix just one dish: soup or squash. They used to eat three times a day, but I couldn't help out with the cooking because there wasn't much of anything to cook.

My father-in-law was really good to me because he was the one who got us together, and he tried to make things work out in every way he could. But I never got to know the family very well, or Warren either. Warren was not bad looking, but it was his way of doing things. He just took me, and he was pretty mean with me.

When I wanted to go home for a visit, my folks would come for me in the buggy. I would stay in Lodge Grass for two or three weeks, and then I had to go back to Warren's house. Whenever I got lonesome, I'd go back home. One time I refused to go back to Warren's place, and my folks knew I was very unhappy, but they encouraged me to go back to Warren and try to work it out. Warren's parents wanted me to come back, and his father tried hard when we were together. But I had made up my mind never to go back, and I never did. If he had been good to me, I now believe I might have stayed with Warren. Later on, when I got acquainted with him, I came to like him a little. But he was mean and jealous, and I couldn't even look around. I stayed with him less than a year. I was pregnant with Bobby three months when I came back to my folks. Bobby was born in 1925. I went to the hospital but got scared and came back home.

John Whiteman's mother and Mrs. Packs The Hat, who adopted me in the Tobacco, delivered Bobby and took care of me. They had me kneel and hold on to something, and I did not cry out, as that's what they expected of women at this time.

One time when our son, Bobby, was six and was going to start school, Warren did come after me. He said, "If you come back with me now, we can start all over and send our boy to school." I said I wouldn't, because I didn't like him, and I didn't think he would ever change. That was the end, because I told him not to come around again and that he would never get me back.

After Bobby was born, I took sick with ulcers and couldn't take care of him. When he was about eight months old, my sister, Amy, took over his care, and in time she and her husband, John, adopted him. Finally I got well, but I didn't care about getting married again. I had decided that all men were mean, and I was afraid to try it again. Besides, my sister, Amy, told me that men didn't like stepchildren and that I shouldn't take Bobby back. She and her husband sent him to school. My brother Robbie and his wife, Lillian Bull Shows, helped buy clothing for him, and Lillian also made clothes for him. Bobby was my only child, and I was never able to have any more. I thought about marrying someone who would like my child, but at the time I was afraid my sister was right about men and stepchildren. I now know that some men can love their stepchildren. Later, my second husband, Donnie, told me, "I would have taken Bobby as my own."

I saw Bobby often when he lived with Amy, for they didn't live very far away. When Bobby was old enough, he went into the marines, and when he came back, he stayed with me until he got married; he never went back to stay with my sister. It is a sad story, but Bobby was always nice and a good son to me.

Marriage to Donnie

I met my second husband, Donnie Deernose, when I was chaperoning Joy, my brother Robbie's oldest daughter. Donnie's brother Jack had gone to Bacone College in Oklahoma, and there he had a good friend named Alvin Warren, a Chippewa Indian. Alvin was a good Christian boy, and he asked Donnie to be a chaperone for him and Joy. That's how we met each other and got acquainted. Robbie would not let Joy go out alone, and so all during the summer months Donnie and I went everywhere with them.

Donnie and I became sympathetic with each other, for each of us had been forced to marry someone we really didn't like. We both had an interest in the young people in the church, and we kept seeing each other. Donnie was a real gentleman, and I couldn't help liking him a lot. We went out together and carried on the church work with the young people for two years before deciding to get married. By that time my dad was gone, passing away in 1927, and that left only my mother to tell about my marriage.

Donnie and I got married in 1931. I was free of Warren, and Donnie's lawyer arranged his divorce from Julie Shafer in that same year. Julie and Donnie were married about four years, but they didn't stay together much. They had three children, and all passed away before they were old enough to go to school.

The Crow Indian preacher at Pryor, John Frost, married us. John Glenn was best man, and we had two witnesses on both sides. Mrs. Frost was there, too. We were married in the Baptist church at Lodge Grass, and I wore an elk-tooth dress given by Donnie's clan aunt, Annie Big Day. Later, I gave this wedding dress to Robbie's wife, Maggie, and she took it to the grave when she passed away. Besides the dresses with the bone elk teeth, Donnie's relatives gave us blankets. All my brothers gave Donnie a horse out of respect for their brother-in-law.

Getting a Start On Our Own Home

We moved in with Donnie's folks at Crow Agency and stayed with them for two years. My health wasn't very good, and I was on a strict diet, almost all vegetables. Donnie managed to get what I needed, and I mixed it up. But his folks, and especially his little sister, liked it and ate it up on me. That was when Donnie built a little house next to his folks and went to work in the government flour mill in Crow Agency. We didn't have very much, and Donnie wanted to farm and raise cattle. In about three years we moved back near Reno to his mother's place where he was raised. About this time his parents moved permanently to Crow Agency.

In getting a fresh start on the farm, we got some help from my relatives. My brother Tom gave Donnie a pig and fourteen chickens. Donnie's adoptive mother, Other Buffalo, gave us a roan milk cow. We had the horses given at our marriage and made a team of them to put in a garden close to the house. We didn't have much ground and had only a little walking plow. Donnie held the plow and I walked the horses, but when we got through it looked rough, so Donnie had us plow crosswise! We finally got the ground soft and put in corn, potatoes, cucumbers, and squash.

Donnie's father, John Deernose (Rides Alongside). Courtesy
Hardin Photo Service.

Donnie got a job hauling logs, and we moved up into the Big Horn Mountains for a couple months. The tribe was building quite a few log houses because they had buffalo there and needed houses for the caretakers. One group they called Hunter's Cabin and the other Aspen Grove.

We camped out with a few other families until it turned cold. That year the winter turned real cold, and we decided to put up ice for use during the summer. We had no refrigerator or icebox. Ice on the river got about a foot thick, and we cut it up in blocks. Donnie hitched up a team and sleigh and hauled the ice and piled it up in a shed. When the weather got warm, we had no ice! After working so hard to get the ice put up, we didn't realize it needed to be covered with straw.

Without the help we got from neighbors and relatives I don't know how we could have made out. Donnie had no car at the time, but I had a Ford. There was a Crow woman married to a White man who used to ask me to drive her to Matt Tschirgi's grocery store. Tschirgi was a big rancher, and the woman leased her land to him. She bought groceries at the store and charged them on her lease money. She always filled up my gas tank and also told me to get a few groceries we needed. For one thing, I'd buy butter. They had sheep, and she gave me some meat from time to time. Her husband, Jim Wilson, had Donnie bring a load of coal from the mine up in the Wolf Mountains. Donnie would leave early in the morning with his team and wagon, and Jim would give him money for coal for them and also for us. Those people really helped us out.

We gave up living at his mother's place and moved to Wyola on land belonging to my brother Carson. He had two places and said we could live in one of them. We put up hay for him. We picked up a team and mower from a ditch rider who lived across the road. Donnie got a loan from the agent and bought the team and mower for four hundred dollars. We also bought an incubator and raised chickens right in the house. Dick Pickett watched the incubator for us.

Our next move was to the old family place where I grew up. Robbie lives there now. We took care of fifteen milk cows for Robbie with the help of Jayhawk, an Ojibwa hired hand. We sent the milk and cream to Sheridan and got our own butter and cream that way. We also raised a lot of chickens with the incubator, and we had a big garden. We stored enough potatoes to last us all winter and bought very little, and I canned vegetables. You wouldn't say we were independent, but we lived comfortably.

The last move was to my grandmother's place here in Lodge Grass, where I now live. We came here during the war, as Donnie always wanted to get close to the river so we would have water for raising stock.

With his father's help, Donnie cleared away all the brush and built a two-room shack with a tar-paper roof and siding. In a few years we added another room, but we needed a larger place. Donnie owned some eighty acres about a quarter-mile from here that he got from his mother. The land belonged to his mother's brother, Billy Steals The Bear, and she got it after he passed away. With the help of his younger brother, Jack, and friends, Donnie dug out a basement and then brought Billy Steals The Bear's house over here. That was in 1952, and over the years Donnie made improvements, including an inside toilet. We started to go automatic around 1960 with a deep freeze. We kept using a wood and coal stove because my mother, who lived with us, cooked as long as she was able. She didn't like the gas and electric stoves because they gave off no heat to warm her. Toward the end she got kind of careless, and we had to watch her, as she was always cold and wore a blanket. We were afraid that when she took the lid off the stove the flame would catch her shawl. "Before she catches fire," Donnie said, "let's take the wood stove out." But Mother didn't like it and complained about the cold, so we built a fireplace and had a fire every evening. She enjoyed the fire, sitting as close as she could. Later we bought an automatic washer.

Donnie was always looking for ways to make life better for us. I think he remembered how his father had told him that the days were gone when the Crows did not have to attend school or train to earn money to put food on the table and clothes on their backs. Even before we were married, Donnie worked hard and learned how to handle money. When his father took sick, Donnie came back from a mechanic's school and took over the farming. One year he got $1,500 for wheat he raised. His folks asked him what he'd like to do with the money, since the check from the sales was made out to him. He told them he'd like to buy a car, and they told him to go ahead. He paid $600 for a Chevrolet touring car and gave the rest to his parents. He kept out $75 so he could take his two brothers, Jack and Winfield, to the Billings Fair and show them a good time. Donnie always respected his parents and family and always wanted to help them.

The War Years

During the war, under Donnie's management, life improved for us, but we worked hard to make a living. We did get some lease money from three sawmills located on our lands. With water pumped from the Little Big

Agnes's mother at one hundred years old. Courtesy Hardin Photo Service.

Horn River next door to us, we had the biggest and best garden in the area. In the summer we put up hay, and Donnie often put off cutting his own so he could cut for others. I worked right along with him, getting up at four in the morning, and then I cooked dinner when we got home in the evening. Donnie was on the stack, Jack worked the fork, and I backed the truck to lift the stacker to where Donnie could reach the hay. We never baled hay at that time. Sometimes Donnie hired Crow friends and relatives, and we'd go to Wyoming to cut and stack hay for extra money.

Early in the war in 1942 we learned they were short of help in the fruit country. Donnie had a big truck with a rack, and we put a tent on it. He took anyone who wanted to go to Toppenish in Washington. We took about twenty people and picked a lot of fruit. They put us in a big tent house, and each family roomed separately. We stayed two weeks and worked every day, but Donnie and I had to return home because of our pigs. Donnie had several hundred pigs, and we left Bobby and Clifford Pretty On Top to watch them. Winona and Ferale took care of the house and chased the pigs out when they got into the house. Bobby and Clifford wrote us to come home because they were running out of food for the pigs. The rest of the Crows stayed all summer, and some of them stayed on and worked there all during the war. But we had so much work to do at home that we couldn't go back. Then, right after we got back, one of Donnie's brothers passed away.

I never liked raising pigs because we always had to watch that they didn't get into our garden. Then one day the pigs did get in and really messed up our planting. After that, Donnie took out a loan and went into cattle. We still raised chickens, and Dick Pickett took care of the incubator. At that time we had about five hundred chickens, some turkeys, and three milk cows.

During the war years the Crow used the Shoshoni Sun Dance to fast and pray for husbands, sons, and grandsons who were in the war. When they first had the Sun Dance, it was new to me and interesting. We used to go and camp, and Donnie helped out with the singing. Donnie liked to sing, and they sang all night. He even went to Fort Washakie for a Sun Dance. But they kept adding things, so that Donnie never cared about going to it anymore. For some reason, toward the end of the war, he turned against it and never bothered to go to it when they had it right here in Lodge Grass in 1975.

Bobby's Wedding

The war affected many of us. My Bobby, Joe Medicine Crow and Arliss Whiteman (Amy's sons), and Jiggs (Robbie's boy) all went off to war. Whenever the soldiers came back on furlough, we had a giveaway for them and invited their clan uncles and aunts to pray for them. We fed them well and wished them good luck while they were gone.

After the war, the Crow put on a big district celebration here in Lodge Grass and had a big giveaway. Just about everybody took part, chipping in something to show their appreciation for the soldiers. Of course, not all of them came home, but luckily we lost only a few.

When our own soldier boys came home, Amy and I would get the Yellowtail and Whiteman relatives together. We'd make the soldier boys go to church first, before having the giveaway. We gave the missionaries something for all their prayers. We had a big giveaway for Bobby when he came home on furlough. Bobby also got married to Clara at that time.

Bobby's marriage was a big affair, and Dr. Petzoldt came. We put up a tent and a tipi for Bobby and Clara and filled it with blankets, a dresser, a bed, pillows, a table, and dishes. There was also a Navajo rug, a beaded robe, and seven elk-tooth dresses for her sisters, as well as beaded belts and buckskin dresses. There must have been forty or fifty pieces of dress goods and head scarves. We dressed the bride in an elk-tooth dress and put her on a horse with an Indian saddle. She got all the wedding saddles I got when I married Donnie. We put her and Bobby on a horse and had them parade. Dr. Petzoldt married them right here at this place, and there must have been a hundred people who came. After the wedding we had a big feast. On Clara's side her mother and father were gone. Clara's clan aunts, Mable Pretty On Top and Lucy Turns Plenty, took care of her relatives' interests. They got all they wanted for themselves. I think Clara kept the tipi.

After the wedding, Bobby had about ten days left. Then he went overseas right away and fought at Iwo Jima. He was wounded and got a Purple Heart. Crow boys, when they returned, were hungry for Indian food, like dry pounded meat. We would fill a one-pound coffee can when they went back to the army, and they would share it with the White boys. The White boys liked it, too.

After the War: Finding an Alternative to Farming

After the war, Donnie and Jack teamed with Arliss Whiteman, their nephew, to purchase a threshing machine, and they traveled around threshing wheat and alfalfa. Lifting sacks weighing 100–150 pounds was hard on Donnie, and one year he came down with hemorrhoids. They were so bad he couldn't work and had to have an operation at a clinic in Excelsior Springs, Missouri. We had been getting along real good with the cattle, but then the doctor told him he couldn't ride a horse or a tractor. So we sold all the cattle, and while he was getting better, we visited Indian tribes in New Mexico and in California. Donnie's sickness forced us to find another way of making a living. We did have lease money, but it wasn't much. For about a year and a half Donnie worked as a maintenance man for Public Health (U.S. Department of Health, Education, and Welfare, Public Health Service Division of Indian Health). Then he picked up some dirt-moving equipment and for several years hired help for excavation jobs and for graveling roads on the reservation.

We had an old friend, Jimmy Thompson, who came and lived with us at this time. He was just like one of us. If he had anything, it was just like ours. Jimmy was a photographer from back East, and he drew a comic strip called "Red Man," which appeared in newspapers all over the country. He used Crow Indians as models for his characters in the cartoons. One time he drew Ataloa and Ferale as princesses who had been separated from their tribe and their many adventures before getting back to their people.

Jimmy and Joy, Robbie's daughter, went everywhere together, and Donnie and I chaperoned them. They wanted to get married, but Robbie was very opposed to it. Jimmy had lived with us before the war, and when he went back East in 1942 he married a teacher from the Lodge Grass Elementary School. They separated after-

Joy, daughter of Robert Yellowtail, and Agnes. Courtesy Hard-in Photo Service.

wards, and Joy, who married a Cherokee Indian, was killed later in an automobile accident.

Jimmy came back to the Crow in 1950 and lived with us. He realized he was very ill and wanted to return and be with the Crow Indians when he died, for he knew we would take good care of him. But he didn't stay long this time because he had an enlarged heart and needed hospital care. At the hospital in Billings they put him in an oxygen tent, and we used to go and visit him almost every day. We were visiting him one day, and Donnie wanted to go out and eat. By the time we returned, after that little time, Jimmy had passed away. We felt just terrible. We kept Jimmy for six days trying to locate some of his relatives but couldn't locate any. Donnie bought his Nash car and used the money to pay his hospital bills. Jimmy was buried in Billings.

American Indian Days

Donnie was a great singer of Indian songs as well as Christian hymns. He used to travel around to Indian powwows in Gallup, New Mexico, with a group of Crow dancers. During the filming of *The Big Sky* he was in charge of the Indians and received $1400 for working forty-two days. He was the one who organized the Indians for a couple other pictures by Paramount. Because of his friendliness and interest in Indian ceremonies, a Mr. Sinclair came to him for help in organizing Indian Days at Sheridan, Wyoming.

Mr. Sinclair had gone to Harvard and studied business administration. He must have liked the West, because he did some ranching on the Crow Reservation and had fun putting on rodeos. We knew him by his nickname, Neckyoke Jones. He first came to our place to

Donnie and dance troupe. Front row, left to right: Joe Medicine Crow, Donnie Deernose, and Henry Old Coyote. Second row, left to right: Tom Yellowtail and Reginald Laubin (non-Indian).

photograph Miss Yellow Mule, who was the first Indian winner of the Sheridan Rodeo Queen contest. In talking with Donnie, Mr. Sinclair got the idea for American Indian Days. This was in 1952, and at first Donnie didn't like the idea, but then he consented to "carry the pipe" to the Indian tribes and invite them to take part. He served as chairman for over twenty years and was a kind of supervisor of all the Indian participants, so we always had a special camping place. I never was in charge of anything, but I helped out with the dancing. At the encampment they gave out rations to the Indians, and one time we got buffalo meat from the Crow tribal herd. At first, American Indian Days was held in conjunction with the Sheridan Rodeo, but it didn't work out, and after that they planned a separate Indian celebration.

We made many new friends through American Indian Days, especially with other Indians from the West, like the Pendleton Indians. They really helped out a lot, bringing their tipis, buckskins, and beaded stuff. Alex Wesley, a Yakima and Nez Percé, became one of our best friends. On Washington's Birthday the Nez Percé put on a big powwow, and for a number of years they invited Miss Indian America to attend. Donnie and I always were the chaperones.

The girls who were contestants for Miss Indian America always liked to talk with Donnie because he was so friendly. He was just like a dad to them. Almost every Miss Indian America used to stay in Sheridan until the next American Indian Days. They weren't used to staying with Whites and would get lonesome. We would invite them to a dance, and they stayed with my adopted daughter, Ferale, and her husband, Bill. We had two Miss Indian America at our last Crow Fair, and they usually come back every year to visit at fair time.

Indian girls from the Southwest always liked to make fry bread, and they liked hot stuff, especialy peppers. Yakimas enjoyed Indian pudding, carrots, bitterroot, and fish. Their favorite foods were fish, huckleberry pudding, and bitterroot; I also liked those foods. I used to get bitterroot from my friends, but they are kind of stingy now. I still have a little and am saving it for special occasions.

There was always a nice worship service at American Indian Days. The men dressed up in warbonnets and the women in buckskins. It made no difference what church you were in, and all came and sat together in the grandstand. Sunday service was the best. They put an organ in the grandstand and had a choir from Sheridan, and we brought our choir from Lodge Grass. The Indian girls made the Lord's Prayer with signs while the others sang it. People liked it, and each year they would get a new Indian preacher.

When Donnie gave up the chairmanship, he suggested that Bill Pease become the next chairman of the American Indian Days Board, and Bill served for three years. American Indian Days was a part of our life right up until Donnie passed away.

Tour of Europe

The best thing that happened to us was a European tour. A friend of ours, Mr. Reginald Laubin, was a writer, and he and his wife made a study of Indian dances. He got in touch with us during American Indian Days in September 1952 to see if we would take part in a performance of American Indian dances in different European countries. During the next summer we practiced our dances for about three months. Some of our dancing partners came from other tribes and camped close by.

We flew from Billings, Montana, to New York and then went by boat to Oslo, Norway. The boat took nine days to get there, and none of us Indians got sick, but some White folks did. In Oslo we visited the sister of a Norwegian man from New York that we adopted as a "son" during an American Indian Days celebration. The Norwegians were very friendly, and I noticed the big bags the ladies carried for shopping. One lady reached into her bag and pulled out a scissors, cut the pear she was eating in half, and gave it to me.

We Crows made up eight of the twelve dancers. The Indians made out the dance program, along with their boss, a Mr. Irwin Harris. They had us put on a few traditional Indian dances. The tour lasted six months, and we danced in fourteen different countries—Norway, Sweden, Finland, Denmark, Belgium, France, Italy, Spain, Switzerland, Portugal, Luxembourg, Israel, Algeria, and Morocco. We traveled through Germany but didn't give any performances there. The ruins in Rome were interesting, and I was happy that we got to see where Jesus was born and lived.

We stayed in Paris one whole month, and every night we noticed a man with a beard wearing a huge cape watching the dancing from the front row. He looked really different to us. One day while shopping we ran into him, and we got acquainted. His wife was pretty and young, and we thought she was his daughter. They invited us to visit them in Switzerland, and during our week's stay in Geneva, they let us use their apartment and showed us around Geneva on foot.

For our return, Lodge Grass District planned a big welcome dance with lots of food, but we came back a day late and missed it. We did make the welcome feast at the church, and they held special prayer meetings for us.

While we were away, we wrote home often. Mother cut a strip of cardboard and marked each day, and I still have that. She was always trying to keep up with things and asked to have the radio on all the time. She didn't know English, but she seemed to know when the news was on. I can see her yet, running to get Ataloa or Ferale, pushing them in front of the radio, and making them listen until the news was over. Then they would tell her what was going on.

Mother always was pretty spry and sometimes sly. She had blue eyes and light skin, and she always wore two pair of stockings under her Indian dress, which covered her completely down below her moccasin tops. When she undressed, the kids saw her white skin and wanted to have skin like hers. Crows admire light skin. She told Ataloa and Ferale when they were kids that she kept herself well covered and never let the sun get at her skin. If they did the same, they could have white skin. The girls decided to get rid of their brown look by covering up their legs, but it didn't work. Mother also told us not to use soap, for that would dry our skin and make wrinkles.

Mother never let me continue in school, yet later on she said that she regretted that she had no education and couldn't speak English. She picked up a little, and she told visitors in English where we were dancing during the European tour. Her other regret was that she never learned to drive a car.

Fixing Up Our Home

Donnie and I saved all the money we could from our European tour, and when we got back we got some

Donnie and Agnes's home, 1986

money from the sale of gravel to the highway committee. With this money we added another room to our house. This really is Donnie's house. I think we put about $8,000 into our house, and Donnie hoped to add central heating for another $2,000. We started with a one-room shack, then a two-room house with a lean-to kitchen, and now, by adding on we have a seven-room house with three bedrooms and two bathrooms. We also have a root cellar to store our vegetables and canned things.

Donnie and I worked hard and earned it by ourselves, for we got very little help from his folks and mine. Donnie used to say, "I never want you to say, 'This money is mine.' If you have money, it is mine also; and if I have money, it is yours." He never could understand his brother Jack and his wife, Fannie. They each had their own money and bank accounts. They did this because

Fannie at first had given her lease money to Jack. But when her children by another marriage wanted money, and she sent them to their stepfather, Jack refused to give it to them. After that Fannie kept her own money.

Donnie never did like to work for wages, although at times he did so. He had a good reputation. When he leased his land to Whites on a year-to-year basis, he never signed anything; it was just a verbal agreement. That was the way it was with the Indian encampment at the Sheridan Rodeo. They knew he could be counted on to be there with his group on time. He never had any trouble getting loans from his White friends. He had many White friends, and one, including a grand potentate, offered to sponsor him in the Blue Lodge of the Masons. He didn't take his friend up on that, but he was a member of the local Lions Club.

Politics and the Yellowtail Dam

Donnie was active in tribal affairs and served as secretary of the Crow tribal council for one term. He wanted to be free to express his opinions and to challenge programs that were bad for the tribe. He served as a tribal delegate to Washington three times, and this led him to study the old treaties and how law applied to Indian legislation. He used this legal knowledge to challenge his opponents in the council meetings. His interest in Indian law led him to join the National Indian Congress in 1951, and he also became a member of the Arrows. The Arrows was a White-sponsored organization working with the National Indian Congress. What Donnie hoped to put across to the Crow was the importance of owning and holding on to their own lands. Crow forefathers fought hard for our land, he said, and kept it for us against the People-who-cut-off-our-heads—the Sioux—as well as the Piegan, Arapaho, and Cheyenne.

In 1956 the question of the Yellowtail Dam split the Crow into two opposing parties. The "adjacent areas" wording in the contract raised the old fear that the government was free to extend land for the damsite clear to the Wyoming line. The Mountain Crow Club was organized to oppose the dam, and the River Crow Club was for it. Bill Russell of Lodge Grass headed the Mountain Crow party, while Posy Whiteman and Bill Wall of Pryor were leaders of the River Crow bunch. Both of these clubs were organized early in May of 1956.

The Mountain Crow held a prayer and thanksgiving meeting as a blessing-wish for a veto of the dam bill on June 9, a Saturday. Donnie and my brother Robbie were the main spokesmen. We had a large crowd of several denominations, including people from the Assembly of God and from the Catholics. Donnie wanted the emphasis to be religious, but Robbie gave a strong political talk. The River Crow had their meeting in Pryor about the same time.

The Big Horn River dam issue put people on different sides, and the Whites got into it, too. One owner of a grocery store in Crow Agency was cussing all over the place because he had lent out $20,000 on credit, counting on the per capita payments the Crow would have with the sale of land for the dam. In the end he didn't have to worry, because the River Crow won out and the dam was built.

While Donnie was working for Public Health in graveling roads and excavating, some friends and relatives, clan brothers, came and asked him to work for the people as tribal secretary. He relied on the advice of his clan uncles, especially Yellow Brow and Jim Blain. They were of the same clan as his father, the Greasy-inside-the-mouth clan. So Donnie ran and was elected in 1964.

John Wilson was chairman at that time, and he and Donnie decided that they would do their best to carry out resolutions of the tribal council. They worked with the executive and agenda committees to draw up resolutions to bring before the council.

Two big issues led friends and relatives to ask Donnie to run for secretary. The tribe was trying to get a settlement on the 107th boundary survey between the Northern Cheyenne and Crow reservations. The original surveyors had given a mile-wide strip of land to the Cheyenne that the Crow felt rightfully belonged to them. Congress held several hearings, but nothing was done, and the matter still isn't settled. There also was talk of building a canal on the west side of the Big Horn River in connection with the proposed Yellowtail Dam. Discussion was heavy because most of the land needed for the canal was owned by the Crow, and they didn't want to have to pay for most of the construction and maintenance costs.

Donnie never was a politician, and he made some enemies when he wouldn't break rules laid down by our constitution. He had problems, too, with people who wanted to be appointed to committees for pay. Some began to put out stories about him, and this led Donnie to hold back on taking a strong position on public issues. When people came to him for advice, he gave them information on both sides of the question and told them to decide for themselves what was best for the tribe and their families. He never took any kind of bribe to influence people and was always honest and fair.

At the end of the term, Donnie filed to run again for tribal secretary, but because of the tactics of his opposition, he decided not to go out and campaign, and he was defeated. The election was not conducted fairly in the way the election judges and clerks were selected and in their regulation of the election. John Wilson protested, but nothing was done to bring about a recall election.

Although Donnie never ran for another office, he kept working on tribal affairs. He was elected as a representative of Lodge Grass District on the Crow Industrial Development Commission, and in 1974 he became chairman. He also was on the utilities commission, which was started to develop programs to protect the health of our district communities, like the sanitation project for Pryor District. He also had a part in the Indian Action Program. With this they hoped to train Indian boys in mechanical and heavy construction work, carpentry, and even motel management. During this time Donnie and I served as counselors for Cheyenne who had become problem children. Donnie wanted to put in four years to make up his Social Security. He applied and got the counselor's job at St. Labre, a Catholic mission and school.

In 1970 they built the Sun Lodge Motel south of Crow Agency with a swimming pool, tipi village, and race track. They wanted to attract tourists, but it didn't work out; the motel and Indian village are getting run-down. The motel management hasn't worked out, but the commission did get a government grant of about $394,000 to renovate the lodge. Under Donnie's leadership they set up a forty-acre industrial site at Crow Agency and constructed buildings that were rented to an electronics company and to a carpet manufacturing company. Neither one worked out for long, but the carpet company lasted eight years.

Bringing Up Our Adopted Children

Donnie and I never had any children, but my mother, Donnie, and I brought up three adopted children. The girls belonged to my mother's brother, and the boy was the first child of my own Bobby. My mother adopted Ataloa when she was about eight months old, before her mother passed away in the hospital in 1930. The other daughter, Ferale, was about two years old at the time. I didn't take her until she was four years old because her dad was living with his first wife's mother, Pretty Shield. I took Ferale one year before I married Donnie, when I was twenty-two years old.

Donnie and I had Ferale for two years when her father, George Hogan, asked me to take her for our own. He was single and was staying with Donnie and me. One day he said, "Why don't you legally adopt her? I will never be able to take care of her. She's young now and will be starting school. If it were a boy, it would be different." So we adopted her with papers, and George soon left to marry Lillian Bull Shows, who had left my brother Robbie. He had two more girls by Lillian before he passed away. Ferale was a spoiled child when we got her, and I knew George didn't always like the way we corrected her.

At the time Mother adopted Ataloa, she was about sixty-five years old and lived in a little house out in back. It was not too long after my father died, and she was in mourning in the old way. She raised Ataloa and taught her how to sew and cook until Donnie and I were able to take both my mother and Ataloa into our home. That was the year the war started, and Ataloa was in the seventh grade. By adoption, Ataloa belonged to my mother's clan, the Whistling-waters, and the same was true for Ferale, since I also was a Whistling-water.

Ataloa and Ferale both finished high school. We made them do their homework every evening. Ataloa became a nurse, and Ferale became a medical secretary. Ferale took sick with tuberculosis, and we had to send her away for one and a half years to a sanatorium in Washington, where she was able to continue her schooling.

I brought Ferale up the best way I could. I showed both Ataloa and Ferale how to help with the housework before they even started to school. Before they left for school, I had them make their beds and do the dishes. I wanted them to be neat and not leave their clothes lying around. I also taught them the Crow language and told them about their clan relatives, both through the mother's and the father's clans. Donnie always told people that they should not be ashamed of being Crows and that they should learn their own language. It made him mad when they didn't. He was especially upset when Ferale and Ataloa didn't teach their children the Crow language.

Donnie always advised Ferale to help people in need. He used to say to her, "If you help them, don't turn anyone down." He also told her that if anyone came into her house, even if she only had dry bread, she should give them some. "Share whatever you have, and when they leave, they will wish you good luck in their hearts." Donnie never liked to ask visitors if they wanted to eat, so he told Ferale just to go ahead and set the food in front of them. This was the way he was taught by his father, Deernose. We tried to get the children to see that each one, in doing something for the family, would be working with the others and would enjoy being togeth-

er. We told them to look for ways to help. Donnie and I
didn't just talk, but we tried to set the example, helping
out, going to church, sharing, and showing respect to
our elders.

Both Ataloa and Ferale were good in their studies,
behaved well in school, and helped me with the house.
Sometimes Ferale would say, "You stay in bed and I'll get
breakfast." We didn't have to punish the girls much, and
even today Crows do not like to whip their children.
There was the one time when Ferale sassed Donnie, and
he took off his belt and switched her, and she never did it
again. I thanked him for doing it, and I told the kids that
Donnie was the head of the family and they should show
respect for him. We tried not to punish our children but
advised them the best we knew how and got them into
church activities. I always told Ferale what my father
had told me about what was good and what was bad.

Donnie was the one who gave permission to stay
overnight at a friend's home. We always told the girls not
to accept rides or any offers of money. We didn't let
Ataloa and Ferale go out very much and told them if their
boyfriends wanted to see them, the boys should come to
our house. If they wanted to see a show, we took them.
We knew that kids like a good time, so we let Ferale go to
the school dances, but we took her and brought her
home. One of Ferale's boyfriends was from North Dakota. He was one of Donnie's Hidatsa relatives, and he and
Ferale wanted to get married. I said that I would not give
permission for their marriage because he was a strong
Catholic and Ferale was a strong Baptist, and that it just
would not work out. People were pretty prejudiced in
those days, not like it is today.

Ferale then started going with Bill Pease, and we got to
know him. He went to church and was a nice boy. He

always came here to see her. I always said to myself, "If I ever have a daughter, she's going to bring her boyfriend here so I can get to know him." What I went through was not good. When they wanted to get married, Bill was the one who asked us and not a relative, according to the old way.

Ferale's Marriage

We found Bill to be just about the nicest boy around. He drank sometimes, but not a lot. He was going into the army, and he and Ferale wanted to get married before he went. When he asked Donnie, Donnie approved. Ferale told Bill to talk to Donnie first, and then she came and talked to me. This was the way she planned it, and after Donnie and Bill talked the marriage over, Donnie thought Bill was about the best boy around here.

I wanted to give Ferale a nice wedding at the church as I had promised her earlier. This meant that they couldn't get married before Bill went into the army. When Bill came back on furlough, they were married by Dr. Petzoldt. We didn't send out wedding invitations because there was no time. There weren't many at the wedding, just his folks and a few friends. Ferale and Bill didn't go on any honeymoon since that is not our custom. Ferale was nineteen at the time.

In the Indian way, I made a buckskin suit for Bill. I got my sister, Amy, to go with me way up into the Big Horn Canyon, off the road, so I would have quiet to do my beadwork. We camped about a week, and I finished the buckskin shirt and pants. I didn't give them a tipi, but I think Ferale got one at a pawnshop in Hardin. Donnie bought a saddle to go with a hat, boots, and a horse. We made Bill parade showing the people what we had given.

Bill and Ferale Pease

Donnie also gave Bill a warbonnet, one of several Donnie had had given to him by his Hidatsa relatives. Today you can dress up a son-in-law with a warbonnet, even if he hasn't been to war. My grandson Leonard never went to war, and he wears one.

Bill's folks were Indians, but not like us. They were what we called "mixed breeds," so they didn't have Indian stuff to give. Ferale didn't get any wedding gifts or anything from his parents, but Bill's mother gave her a shower in the White man's way.

In our way a son-in-law doesn't talk to his mother-in-law. Even before Bill married Ferale, I told him that I would not talk to him once they got married. I was just teasing, but he felt bad about it and didn't like the idea of not talking to me. So we decided not to follow the Indian way. I gave him a beaded belt to go with his buckskin outfit for the right to talk to him. Then I had the crier announce it at a public gathering. I also visited his folks, and we used to ask them to come over and eat with us.

Ferale and Bill never lived with us after their marriage. She and Bill spent about five years in Browning, four at Poplar, and about five at Fort Washakie. After that they were transferred back here, as he worked for the Bureau of Indian Affairs.

Grandson Duane

The marines sent my son, Bobby, home after he was wounded at Iwo Jima. He and Clara stayed here for a while, and then Amy and I gave Bobby land that belonged to my father and his brother, Robert Rises Up. The land was about nine miles from here toward the mountains. My father willed part to me and part to Amy, and we each gave our share, which was about 130 acres of farmland. Bobby borrowed some money from the government and bought some tractors, and they did real well for quite a few years. He had cattle, and he and his neighbors helped each other. By this time Bobby and Clara had ten children, and they built a new house on the land we had given them. Getting the children to school in the wintertime was pretty hard, and so in the winter they stayed with us. Then Bobby sold his cattle, and they moved in with us and stayed for about five years.

Clara breast-fed Duane, my first grandchild, born while Bobby was away in the war. Donnie and I thought that we would keep him while he was being weaned, but we never gave him back. Duane was nine months old at the time, and sometime later Bobby returned from the war.

To wean Duane, we kept him from his mother and gave him soft foods like cereal and milk. Clara didn't have enough milk, so we kept him on a bottle, teaching him how to drink out of a cup. We didn't have baby foods, and as he grew up we fed him mashed potatoes. We could have used Pampers, for it seemed like we washed flannel diapers every day! Clara had a kid almost every year, and she washed on a washboard or in a tub. I used a tub and rubbing board, but later we got a washing machine. It was run by gasoline and was not automatic. My mother had a washing machine that you turned by a handle, and we kids took turns, Tom and I, or whoever was there.

We used Johnson's baby powder and oil when we bathed Duane. Crows have used a baby powder ever since I can remember. In my mother's day they used red earth to clear up rashes and sores. Grandparents on the father's side made a baby cradle for a grandchild and, for the first one, beaded it all over. I never used a cradleboard with Duane, but my nephews, Joe Medicine Crow and William Yellowtail, have used cradleboards with their children.

Duane walked when he was a year and a half. He was always with Donnie, and Donnie was always fixing things at the church. Duane had Donnie's big cowboy hat on, and when Donnie made a motion for him to come, he walked to Donnie. When kids start walking you can't hold them back, and so I made little moccasins for Duane when we took him to church. I didn't want him to make as much noise as some kids do with their hard shoes.

We practically raised Duane in the church. Dr. Petzoldt baptized him when he was about twelve years old. I always thought they took Duane to the river and baptized him with all his clothes on, but Duane said he was baptized in the baptistry at Wyola. Dr. Petzoldt usually baptized in the river, but Duane was afraid of the water so he went to the baptistry. Miss Olds gave Duane a Bible.

Duane always wanted to be with Donnie, for boys always look to men and girls to women. I did talk to Duane and told him what he should do, and Donnie did the same. We taught him to respect other people and his clan uncles. "You should help older people when they need it. You should take them wherever they want to go," we told him. Duane got to know his clan uncles real well. Because his father was a Whistling-water, or Bedekyosha, Duane and all the kids whose fathers were Whistling-waters had the right to tease or make fun of each other when they made mistakes. Duane got his clan from his mother and his teasing relatives from his father's side.

Duane went to school in Lodge Grass. We started him when he was six years old, and he was a good boy in school. He developed a great interest in basketball and football. During his high school days, they had a real good basketball team, and we followed him to the different towns where they played. When he graduated, we didn't have a big giveaway for him but just served cake and ice cream at the church. People didn't have big giveaways at graduation.

Duane continued his schooling at a junior college at Miles City for about a year. Then he went to Dodson College in Glendive, Montana. He took up surveying, borrowing money for his education from the agency, which he is supposed to pay back. We helped him with spending money. During the summer he worked with a survey crew, and he could have continued, but he didn't want to go so far away into Wyoming. He never did go back to work with them. He was about twenty-one at the time. I kept telling him he should try to get a job using what he had learned. I never learned why he didn't want to go with the survey crew, and later on he told me he was sorry he hadn't gone. All of a sudden he volunteered and went in the army, even though there was no war. He trained around Denver but never went overseas. While he was in school, Duane never liked to drink, but he turned that way when he went into the army.

Donnie always wanted Duane to be a mechanic or a carpenter, but Duane was not interested. He wanted to fool around with raising cattle, but we had sold our cattle before his time and so could not help him out there. He never had to pay board and room, and we didn't give him many jobs to do around the house. When we had wood stoves, the boys always brought in wood and coal, emptied the ashes, and brought water. But now we have gas and running water and there isn't much for kids to do except to get in a car and go somewhere. Nowadays we don't handle money for our adopted kids. They know too much now and won't let you do anything with their lease or per capita money.

Duane has been living with us almost all of his life. He never got along with his parents because he never lived with them, and he never got to know his brothers and sisters very well either. This was even though Bobby and Clara raised their children here while they were living with us. Because Duane never got along with his parents and his brothers and sisters, I told Bobby and Clara that I would never adopt another grandchild. Duane is thirty-five years old, and he still doesn't know what he wants to do with his life. But that is true for many of our young people today.

CHAPTER 7

Life Without Donnie, The Complete Bear

The Accident

On a Sunday morning in September 1977, we had an accident that changed our lives. Donnie was driving from church and was just turning into our place when a big semi-truck hit us broadside. The road curves to the right just before the entrance, and it's not easy to notice a car or truck coming in back to pass. The truck hit on the driver's side, spinning us into a slough, which kept us from turning over. The blow bent the car on the driver's side, broke all the glass, and threw Donnie down between the seats. We had a little granddaughter in the back seat, but she didn't get hurt, and except for cuts, I was not hurt either.

I thought Donnie was dead. I rubbed him and called to him, but he had passed out and didn't move. Our other grandchildren saw what had happened and came running, and Duane called the ambulance and patrolman. People in cars behind us stopped and tried to help. When they started to pull Donnie out, a nurse said, "Wait a minute, maybe he is hurt in the back." It was hard to wait, especially when Donnie started to come to and moan, and tell us, "Get me out of here." About that time the patrolman and the ambulance came, and they pulled him out and took him to the hospital in Crow Agency. By the time we arrived at the hospital he was already in intensive care. The doctor said that all the bones on his left side, his collarbone and ribs, were broken. They sent him to Billings in an ambulance, and he stayed there until he was healed enough to be returned to the hospital at Crow Agency. When Donnie finally came home, we had a big picnic and giveaway in back of the church in thanksgiving for his recovery and to thank those who had prayed for him.

Donnie came home in October, but within two months he was back in the hospital because of a blood clot in his head. They drilled two holes on each side and drained that blood off. He seemed to be getting along all right, and we brought him home. But he kept losing weight and didn't get around much. Then one day he said, "I feel a little better," and he thought he would start on the screening of the meat house I had been wanting. When the boys went hunting for elk and deer, I had no place to hang the meat up to cure. While he was working, all of a sudden Donnie didn't feel good, and I took him back to the hospital. We learned that he had an infected gallbladder and they had to operate. He was in the hospital in Billings, and after the operation he was doing real well. The doctor told me that he could go home.

On the very day Donnie was to go home, he complained of chest pains, but the nurse didn't call the doctor. They made him get up and walk and gave him juice to drink. Donnie never got mad very easily, but now he said, "If you don't get the doctor for me, I'll just walk out of here." They called the doctor, and when they gave him a shot, his body turned cold with sweat. So they hurried him into intensive care. I was told to gather up all his belongings and take them with me. While I

was getting Donnie's things together, the doctor came
and said, "If you want to see him, you had better go in. I
don't think he is going to pull through." When I started
to go in the room, Donnie had another attack, and they
pushed me out. The heart specialist said they couldn't do
anything about it because the tubes to the heart were all
plugged up. But if they had got to him right away when he
first complained, Donnie might have pulled through.

The Funeral and Giveaway

They kept Donnie one day in Billings before they took
him to the Bullis Mortuary in Hardin. They kept him in
Hardin for four days before the funeral in the Chivers
Memorial Baptist Church, our church, here in Lodge
Grass. We called around to his friends and the Sheridan
people he had worked with, including his many friends
in the American Indian Days celebrations.

Donnie's funeral was about the biggest the Crows ever
had. We had a wake for him, and his friends wanted to
sit up with him all night. All of his relatives brought me
something for the giveaway. One of his Crow friends
butchered for us, and everybody had enough meat to
eat. The Baptist ladies also prepared seventy pounds of
beef, which they bought from Stevenson's Store in
Lodge Grass. A friend of mine furnished all the other
food, plates, and settings. So the funeral went over big. I
tried to give his friends from out-of-state something to
take back with them. The funeral and giveaway took
place on February 23, 1978.

One of Donnie's best friends from North Dakota
brought a brand new warbonnet for him. We laid out
Donnie's own warbonnet on the coffin, and I was going
to put it away with him. But his friend said, "Take the

Crow Indian Baptist church, Lodge Grass, Montana, 1986

other one back, and put this one I now give you in there. I want to tell you something. It is our Indian custom not to bury the person's warbonnet with him. It's bad luck. Before they bury him, take the warbonnet back. I want you to keep it as a keepsake." My brother-in-law, John Whiteman, told me the same thing. So I took the warbonnets before they carried Donnie up on the hill for burial. If any of my grandchildren want to borrow these warbonnets when they parade, I'll let them have the warbonnets. But I'll take them back and put them away.

Hidatsa people sit up with their dead ones. They have coffee and sandwiches, and if they get tired, they go and get food. The wake goes on all night, and just to sit there is tiring. So I asked different ones to come and hold a little service for him. I knew about the wake before when some of Donnie's relatives passed away and we went there. The Catholics came and read from the Bible and sang hymns and played the guitar. They had many good things to say about Donnie. The Mormon missionary sang "How Great Thou Art" and talked about life and its spiritual existence. Pentacostals also came, and various individuals were invited to give their thoughts about Donnie. Some just got up and said some good words. Bill Russell talked about the Christian quality of Donnie's life and what the Bible taught about life and death. Helen Pease Wolf described how Donnie and I were good examples of a Christian couple, that we were always together at church. There were others, too.

The wake continued until six o'clock in the morning. There were about one hundred and fifty people at the wake, and I think that what the different denominations did helped those sitting there. Our own missionaries stayed up with us and held a service, even though they must have been tired. Toward morning I spoke to Donnie's Hidatsa relatives: "We'll go home and wash and clean up and then come back. You folks come and clean up too." But one of them spoke up, "It's our custom never to leave him alone. When you come back, we'll go." That was something new to me, that someone had to stay with Donnie all the time.

We dressed Donnie in a buckskin suit with a flower design, which I had made earlier as a parade suit for him. He had wanted one with an Indian design, and I finished that in time for the Crow Fair. He wore it only once in the parade. People said I should keep the Indian-design buckskin, so I did. My son, Bobby, wears it now, and it fits him real well.

Donnie's casket was of dark burnished bronze out-lined in gold and with gold handles. They placed the casket in front of the lectern. We put a red-design Pendleton blanket under his shoulders and drew it up on the open lid. We painted two red short lines horizontally from each eye, and we put away with him a shell disc necklace of many strands that had belonged to his father, Deernose, also known as Runs Alongside. He held his father's eagle-feather fan in his right hand. At Donnie's feet we put his Hidatsa friend's warbonnet. Ferale asked me to give her the warbonnet as a keepsake, which I did. Every time some friend or relative came to pay their respects to Donnie, I and my daughter, Ferale, greeted them and took them over to the casket. I couldn't help breaking out weeping, especially with the women, who came with tears in their eyes and some of them sobbing. My sister's daughter, who is like a daughter to me, played hymns on the church organ during the wake.

Monday, the day of the funeral, was a cold and cloudy day, threatening snow. A crowd of nearly six hundred people gathered at the church, some coming from New

Mexico and Illinois. Most Crows who came were from our Lodge Grass District, but some of the tribal officers showed up. The tribal chairman, Forest Horn, did not come, and neither did the secretary.

We left it to the mortician, Bullis, to take care of the funeral part. He brought special stands for a cross of white carnations and another for a cluster of pink carnations. He surrounded the coffin with bouquets, wreaths, and pots of yellow, white, red, and pink flowers. Some of our friends brought potted flowers to me.

Mr. Bullis placed our family and close relatives of Donnie in the first two pews facing the altar. In the first two pews to the right were the pallbearers and honorary pallbearers. Lynn Harris, Marvin Passes, Frank Backbone, Jr., Don Pease, Arnie Bends, and Larry Dean Yellowtail were the casket bearers. The honoraries were Melvin Parsons, Charles DeCrane, Robert Littlelight, Dan Old Elk, Warren Bear Cloud, and Kenneth Yellowtail. Lynn Harris and Marvin Passes were close friends and clanmates of Donnie. Frank Backbone, Jr., was his sister's son. Arnie and Larry were my son's boys, although Larry was adopted by Maggie Yellowtail, Robbie's wife who had passed away. Marvin Parsons, Charles DeCrane, Robert Littlelight, Dan Old Elk, Warren Bear Cloud, and Kenneth Yellowtail were his "children" in the Crow way. Marvin Parsons is chairman of the present board of American Indian Days, and Dan Old Elk was a member of the dancing troupe that Donnie led to Europe in 1973.

Our minister, Morley Langdon, took charge of the funeral service. Minnie Ellen Whiteman, my sister's daughter, played the organ during the preparation, but as the service neared, we had a White girl substitute for her, so she could be with us as a family.

We asked David Stewart (who used to be tribal chairman), Dan Old Elk, and Melvin Parsons to tell about Donnie. David told what an honest person Donnie was, how Donnie had told David that he had not voted for him because he did not think David was qualified to be tribal chairman. Just the same, Donnie worked closely with David when he became chairman, and David said he knew that he had found the right adviser in an honest man. He also pointed out how devoted Donnie was to helping his Crow people, as with his work with American Indian Days and his tours of Europe with the dancers. Donnie brought dignity to Indian ways through his interpretations to Europeans, and his explanations and motions during the peace-pipe ceremony were unforgettable. Stewart spoke first in Crow and then gave a brief English translation, while Dan Old Elk spoke only in Crow. Marvin Parsons had great things to say about Donnie's contributions to the founding of American Indian Days and his services for twenty-four years as chairman. Our missionary's wife ended this part of the service by giving a brief history of Donnie's life and accomplishments.

We had an Indian version of the Twenty-Third Psalm printed on the announcement of Donnie's funeral. It goes like this:

The Great Father above a Shepherd Chief is. I am His and with Him I want not. He throws out to me a rope and the name of the rope is Love, and He draws me to where the grass is green and the water is not dangerous, and I eat and lie down and am satisfied. Sometimes my heart is very weak and falls down, but he lifts me up again and draws me into a good road. His name is Wonderful.

Sometime, it may be very soon, it may be a long, long time, He will draw me into a valley. It is dark there, but I'll be afraid not,

162   *They Call Me Agnes*

for it is between those mountains that the Shepherd Chief will meet me and the hunger that I have in my heart all through this life will be satisfied.

Sometimes He makes the love rope into a whip, but afterwards He gives me a staff to lean upon. He spreads a table before me with all kinds of foods. He puts his hand upon my head and all the "tired" is gone. My cup He fills till it runs over. What I tell is true. I lie not. These roads that are "away ahead" will stay with me this life and after; and afterwards I will go to live in the Tepee and sit down with the Shepherd Chief forever.

During the time when individuals were respecting Donnie's memory with kind testimonials, the mortician had the casket closed. We sang two of Donnie's favorite hymns, and we relatives just burst out in tears at the thought of his going away from us. Mr. Bullis had the casket bearers move the casket to the side door near the front of the church. There, with the lid raised once more, all but close family relatives had a last farewell for Donnie. Some of his friends and clan members, especially the women, touched his hand and kissed his face, breaking out with, "I have lost a friend!" or, "I have lost a brother!" Then it was our turn to say farewell as Mr. Bullis moved the casket to block the doorway. Then we family filed by and sobbed our grief and loss according to our relationships: "I have lost a clan uncle, a brother, a brother-in-law, a father, or a husband!" I asked the minister's wife to stay close to me, and she helped me with a gentle embrace and led me away from the casket. Crows always weep hard on taking a last look at the one who goes on ahead, and grief felt at this time is so deep for some that they need a kind relative to lead them away from the coffin.

We came out of the church to a cold, gray sky and light

snow. The funeral procession of cars passed through the town of Lodge Grass and proceeded up the hill past the school to the cemetery situated at the edge of the bluff. Mr. Bullis had chairs for us at the south edge of the grave.

Donnie belonged to the Big-lodge clan, which is linked to the Newly-made-lodges, and they joined to sing a special song for him. My sister, Amy, sang a special Whistling-water clan song. No one likes to sing the clan song at such a time, for whoever hears it will feel sad. We used to have a club called the Crazy Dancers. They were always ready to help out and to get things going. Most of the members were gone, such as Pretty On Top and Bird In Ground. Those who were left talked about what song they should sing for Donnie and chose a good one. That was the saddest part, and the people started crying. When an outstanding person passes away, they sing a special song for him, and that is what they did for Donnie.

When they began to lower the casket, people could not help but sob and cry out. Long ago, in our old way, close relatives cut off their braids, gouged themselves in the arms, legs, and head to make the blood flow, and in their grief cut off finger joints. Some still were doing that when I was a little girl. Now we just mourn, wearing black like the White folks, although black was and still is our sign of victory and of joy when used in our ceremonies, like the Sun Dance.

Clan brothers took up the shovels to throw the rocky soil upon Donnie's casket. From time to time another clan brother or friend touched the worker and took up the shovel. Cyrus Preston, a Navajo who worked with Donnie on the industrial commission, threw some shovelfuls of earth out of friendship and respect. When only about six inches of earth remained to be filled in, Mr. Bullis arranged the flowers from the church on top of the grave.

Donnie's sister, Stella, used Barney Old Coyote, Jr., as a herald to thank everyone who had come, for she knew how cold it was. Barney couldn't hold back his feelings as he talked about Donnie. And then came the time for our final farewell. My nephew and "son," Joe Medicine Crow, waited for the drummer-singers to strike the drum a heavy blow to sound like the thunder, and then he told how he and Donnie had used the dancing society known as the Rees to retain some of the old songs and ceremonies. They had done this right after the war. When they visited other Crows to enlist their support, they announced their coming by singing a song that a Hidatsa clan uncle of Donnie's had given Donnie on one of his visits to us. The clan uncle was known as Middle Of The River Bear, and Donnie's honor name was The Complete Bear. The song was called "Medicine Lake," a place very sacred to the Hidatsa and to the Crow. This lake is known today as Devils Lake, North Dakota. The song in a way belonged to Donnie, and they were going to sing the song four times and then never sing it again. They buried the song with Donnie.

After the singing of the Medicine Lake Song, the funeral ended, and people broke away to go home or to the church. My son, Bobby, announced that the Pentecostals would hold a special prayer meeting for Donnie on Wednesday evening and that they would provide food.

Back at the church I had a giveaway to honor Donnie, and some of the Hidatsa relatives also had giveaways. I sat next to a table where I had placed a large picture of Donnie. I asked Bobby to announce the names of guests to be honored. Some had performed services by telling about Donnie, or donating beef, or traveling a long distance—like Jimmy King, who came from Colorado, and Fred Voget, who came from Illinois. We honored friends from out-of-state first. I tried to give each one a woolen blanket, a piece of dress goods, or some beaded material. When we served the food, we had the out-of-state friends line up first, and following our custom, the men lined up before the women.

In our Indian custom we Crow usually mourn for one whole year. A widow in mourning used to lose her tipi to relatives and friends who came and took poles, robes, and household equipment. A good relative usually kept some special things for her, like her sewing outfit or a knife. A widow in mourning was not supposed to cook or sew, and she had food brought to her makeshift shelter of branches set up at each camping place. I think they broke up the tipi house because they didn't want the ghost to find his way back.

When they set up the reservation and Indians began living in log and frame houses, Crow mourners couldn't just move out of the house for good or let relatives come and take it apart. Some did move out of the house for a while. When someone was sick and about to pass away, the Crow sometimes put up a tent away from the main dwelling for the sick person. If a person did pass away inside the house, they took the person out as fast as they could through a window, so the ghost could not find its way back very easily. We still bury personal things, but they don't bury sewing machines, axes, tubs, and guns the way they used to when I was growing up. Bloodline relatives of a person have the right to take personal belongings and mementos, such as pictures, photographs, saddles, and horses.

All these customs are slowing down. People don't like

to mourn for a whole year anymore. I mourned for
Donnie six months. His sister Pearl told me, "It's long
enough. He's been gone six months." They wanted me to
come down to Crow Agency for the dress-up ceremony
ending the mourning, but I began crying and said, "It's
too early. It seems like he just passed away." But you are
not supposed to refuse when his relatives tell you, "It's
long enough." So I went to Crow Agency, and Donnie's
sisters—Stella, Pearl, and Ruby—dressed me up in a
buckskin dress and beaded leggings and gave me shawls
to wear that were bright colors and showed that I was no
longer in mourning. His sisters had prepared the clothes
to dress me up. This is how I came to give up mourning
after six months, and then I went to Sheridan where
Crows and other tribes were camping out for American
Indian Days. It's up to relatives to tell you when to stop
mourning. You just can't do it on your own.

It was hard to come back home and live without him.
Where he had sat at the table seemed so empty, and I
couldn't sit down to eat. I would just begin crying and
leave the table. This went on for about a month, and I
never wanted to leave the house. In about a month I did
go to the grocery store in Lodge Grass. My sister, Amy,
and her daughter said, "You're alone. Come and live with
us." But to do that seemed as if I would be leaving
Donnie behind, and I couldn't leave him. We used to go
to North Dakota two or three times each year, and his
relatives invited me to come, but I didn't go. I know that
Donnie thought a lot of his relatives, but if I went
without him, it would not be the same. It has now been
two and a half years since he passed away, and I now feel
like going and visiting our friends in Taos. Gradually I'm
getting over that feeling of loneliness.

I lost my mother and father and brother, but losing

Donnie was the hardest for me. I haven't forgotten him, and I never will. Donnie used to do most of the driving, and when I drove myself to Crow Agency, I would cry all the way down and back. Then one day I said to myself, "The Lord is with me. I am not alone." So now instead of crying, I sing church songs in the Indian way. I knew that I wasn't alone, and that helped me gradually to get over that crying. The church is all I live for now, and church doings are what I look forward to now.

If I were a non-Indian, I would stay here by myself. I'm in a big house, and so I asked my grandchildren not to leave me for two or three years anyway. I still don't like to stay alone. In the daytime it's not so bad, but in the evening I miss my partner. If my grandchildren don't come back during the day, I just go and stay with my "sister," Ataloa, in Lodge Grass. My adopted daughter, Ferale, has invited me to come and stay with them, but I don't know how to stay with other people. Living with others is probably still ahead of me. I could manage if Duane got married and stayed here, but he doesn't stay home long enough. I don't intend to remarry, so it's just going to be this way for the rest of my life. It's really sad when you lose a fine man like Donnie.

Celebrating the Year Together

Seasonal Circles and Celebrations

When I look back on our old ways, I can see that my people, the Absarokee, followed a kind of rhythm in their lives throughout the year. The year made a kind of circle, and the circle, like the sun, was important to the Crow. When they entered and left the tipi, they made a circuit following the sun. That ceremonial circuit continues today when entering the Peyote tipi and the Sun Dance lodge. My brother Tom uses the circle and spokes of a wagon wheel to explain how all religions take different paths to the same Creator.

During buffalo-hunting days, from late fall to early spring people had to break up into small groups to find a sheltered camp near a good wood supply and where they could get buffalo or elk when they needed food. They usually settled in cottonwood groves, and they used the bark of this tree to feed their horses during winter snows. They cut the cottonwood branches into three-to-four-foot lengths, and the horses could hold the branch steady while nibbling at the bark. It wasn't the best, but it saved the horses.

In those old days, the Mountain Crow and the River Crow bands often traveled together from late spring into summer because buffalo were always within reach and food was plentiful. This was a time when Crow people visited as a tribe. They usually got together after the spring planting of sacred tobacco when they could turn their attention to celebrating marriages, holding give-aways, and trying to outbid each other for recruits for the military societies. Sometimes they held a Sun Dance, pledged by a mourner eager to kill as many of the enemy as possible to avenge a brother or father.

When my people moved to the reservation, the old rhythm of life was broken. The old reasons for separating and then getting together ended. But the Crow people were used to doing things together, and by my day they had developed a new rhythm that combined some of our own celebrations with White ones. The ceremonies might be changed to fit in with our own, but the Crow kept a seasonal circle in their living.

Beginning the New Year: The Crow Tribal Fair

As in the old days, Crows begin the New Year with lots of good fun, good-luck wishes, and plenty to eat. We do this with our fair and rodeo held in August at Crow Agency. Sometimes there are over eight hundred tipis. We take bedsprings and rollaway beds to sleep on in tents pitched in back of our tipis. This is a good time for women to sew, cook, and visit. We all dress up in our best parade outfits, and the best ones are given first, second, and third prizes. We parade with our clan, and there are prizes for Indian dancing. Lots of Indians come—Nez Percé, Blackfeet, Bannock, Shoshoni, Chey-enne, and Sioux. We make a big camp of tipis for our guests. They eat well on buffalo meat from our tribal herd, and the most important fair officers are sure to hold giveaways; the fair officers always give presents to the visiting Indians to give them a good feeling when they leave.

When my husband, Donnie, was treasurer of the Crow Fair and John Cummins was president, we had a big giveaway. We gave two or three blankets to each of Donnie's clan uncles and aunts, and then we made all the visitors stand in a circle and we went along the line giving a blanket to each of them, or a scarf, or some dress goods or money. We finished it up that way because we figured that they had come a long way and should have something to take home. We wanted them to be happy, so we gave them everything we had.

Our relatives helped us out at Donnie's giveaway—his mother, my mother, and his sister and brothers especially. Costs were not too bad then, but today a Pendleton blanket costs around eighty dollars; the Crow still give plenty of them, and the tag will still be on them! Crows like to know that they are not getting used stuff, and when you parade at the Crow Fair, you always wear a new blanket and leave the tag on in case one of your relations asks you for it, or admires it—for that is the same as asking. When a clan brother or sister asks for something, or asks by admiring, you just can't refuse.

When you have a giveaway, it's up to your relatives if they want to help. They collect the stuff way beforehand, like my sister, Amy. She had several trunks filled with quilts, about fifty of them, about thirty heavy blankets, and the same number of light blankets, dress goods, and scarves. She was ready when her son's daughter wanted to be adopted into the Tobacco Society. Diane wanted the Tom Big Lakes of Pryor to adopt her, so my sister told the Big Lakes that she wanted to "give" her granddaughter to them. They agreed, and Amy pitched her tipi next to the adoption lodge, and she just about filled the tipi with all those quilts and blankets for the adoption price. Every one of those blankets had been given to her and her husband at giveaways. They never had to go out and buy anthing for Diane's adoption and giveaway. You can count on some relatives putting out quite a lot for you, even giving away a horse or a cow, as well as elk-tooth dresses and beaded stuff.

You always hear a lot of praise songs during the Crow Fair because of the giveaways, for a big gathering is the best time to honor your boy for his achievements. As a Crow you never stand up in public and tell of your successes. We have a herald, or crier, who announces what you have done. This is the time for clan uncles and aunts to sing their praise songs for their clan child.

The Crow have praise songs that are owned by individuals, families, clans, and the tribe. Individual praise songs have been handed down by respected clan uncles and aunts, and that's the way it is with family songs, too. Some elders can use their praise songs to honor a clan child, clan brother, or anyone, but there aren't more than three or four today licensed to sing on all occasions.

Any family member can sing a family praise song to honor himself, his brothers, his brother's children, or his own child. You can use the family praise song when dancing your entrance into a hall with a brother's son who is to be honored with a giveaway. When a veteran honors himself with a giveaway on Soldier Boys' Day, he can sing his family praise song. A clan praise song is used to honor the children of the clan. If some of the sons and daughters of my clan brothers were to give something nice, like a horse, I have a right to sing my Whistling Water clan song for them. Very few women own praise songs, and so Amy and I, as well as our "sister" May Old Coyote, sing our clan song.

In the old days they needed praise songs to honor the young warriors who were always doing great deeds to help their people. Today a crier sings clan praise songs to honor the president and secretary of the Crow Fair, or for any person honored by the clan. Anyone in the clan can request the drummers to sing the clan honor song.

Crows like to put on a feast for clan uncles and aunts before the tribal fair, for they can bring good luck through their dream-blessings to someone in the parade, dance, and rodeo competitions. My brother Carson used to butcher once a year on the Fourth of July. Just before the last Crow Fair, his son, Kenneth, invited me, Amy, Robbie, and Tom to one of these cookouts. Kenneth is like a son to us, and he told us, "This way you'll not have to buy meat during the Crow Fair." Kenneth went on to say, "You're getting old, and I want to show my love for you. When my father was alive, he used to do this, so I'm going to do this as long as you're alive." He didn't have to do that for us. Cattle were high in price, and he could have sold them, but Kenneth did that for us, and we appreciated it very much.

John Whiteman, Amy's husband, sang his praise song for him, and Amy and I wished him blessings for his family and children, and many more days to live. I didn't have any dream-blessings to give, for I never dream of those good things like others do. Some clan uncles and aunts say they dream of new berries, or of threshing wheat—something good that they can give to their clan children to get through to that time of year without bad luck.

We always have a happy time at these cookouts because we get our favorite meats. Crows like fresh liver and kidneys, especially when there's fried bread cooked over the fire, as my mother used to fix it, along with coffee. The whole rib is especially delicious, for Crows put the ribs on sticks and stand them up by the fire to broil. That's really good!

Whenever clan uncles are invited to a feast, they are served special Indian foods. Indian puddings made from buffalo berries, gooseberries, serviceberries, and chokecherries and fry bread are certain to be served, along with dried meat, pounded meat, and pemmican. The women also make *sheboreh*, or sausage, if it is around butchering time. They strip the tenderloin about an inch thick and wide and stuff it in the guts. They turn the guts inside out and put the meat inside with salt and pepper and a lot of water. The guts are tied at both ends with strings. Boiling from five to ten minutes makes a lot of juice, and the juice with the sausage are great favorites.

Halloween

We usually begin our district social get-togethers with a masquerade dance on Halloween. The drummer singers use the small hand drum. Everyone tries to look funny and crazy, like a tramp or a boogeyman. Some men dress as women, and women may dress as men. Everyone wears a Halloween mask bought at a store, and the dancing may get quite hilarious. When they unmask, I'm always surprised at the antics of certain people. There is no feast, but someone is there to sell food. They give cash prizes for the best costume and dancing. Before the Crow took up Halloween, a few men used to disguise themselves with mud masks and ragged clothing and make fun in mock fighting or dancing. Sometimes a man dressed to look like a pregnant woman.

Soldier Boys' Day, Agisaday Eshbaabua

This is another White man's celebration we took over. We had Crow boys in the first war, and when they came home, each district had its own big feast and dance. Relatives honored their soldiers with giveaways.

I went with my father and mother to the first Lodge Grass celebration in 1918. We camped at the Muddy Mouth campground for a couple days while the soldier boys had their giveaways. When they celebrated with a "glad dance," they sang a song, "Iron Hats, we got the best of you!" When they sang this song, the women jumped up and down because they were real happy. Today only Lodge Grass puts on a dance in the evening, and district recreation officers ask people, including veterans, to donate for the feast.

Thanksgiving, or Giving Thanks

Thanksgiving we also borrowed from the Whites, but it was a Crow custom to hold ceremonies to give thanks when cured of an illness or when bad luck turned into good. When I was a girl, we met in the district round hall in Lodge Grass, and each family set a table for first, second, and third prizes. We don't do that anymore, but Thanksgiving was a special time for inviting several clan uncles and aunts to eat their favorite Crow foods, and they wished their clan sons and daughters all good luck until the next Thanksgiving.

Churches also had Thanksgiving services. At our mission church we called it Harvest Home. We'd fix potatoes, fruit, jelly, pan-fried bread, and pemmican, and we baked pies and bread. We took them to the church the night before, and after the church service, we had a feast together. When Dr. Petzoldt retired around 1955, we decided to sell the food to each other and to give the money to the church. We were thankful to God for this food, and that's why we gave the money from the auction to the church.

We have social dances in the evening at all the big celebrations, like Thanksgiving and New Year's. They drum and sing Crow songs and dance the Push and Owl dances. I don't know how many songs Crow men have composed, but it must be three thousand at least, and good drummers and singers know several hundred.

For the dances, women dress up in their best elk-tooth dresses with wide beaded belts and high-topped moccasins made white by brushing them with flour. The men are the ones who really dress up, as that has always been our way. However, today not many men wear the colorful costumes made of long underwear dyed in beautiful reds, maroons, yellows, blues, and blacks that were the fashion when I was young. The little capes hanging down over the shoulders were heavily beaded with our favorite blues, yellows, reds, and whites. They wore wide beaded belts with flower designs and beaded gauntlets to match. They accented their rhythms with a ring of cowbells around their ankles or a streamer of sheep bells stretching from knee to moccasin. All the dancers wore a bustle of feathers in back, usually turkey feathers, because the eagle was a protected bird and their feathers hard to get.

For the Push and Owl dances, four men usually beat on tambourine-type drums and sing. When the men do the war dance, the drummer-singers use a regular marching drum borrowed from the Whites. We call our traditional tambourine drum "Drum-that-makes-noise," and the round band drum "Big Drum."

The Push and Owl are the main dances for women. The Push Dance is our fox-trot. When it started up, they called it the Indian fox-trot or the trotting dance. I don't know how we got that Push name, although a man holds the woman in a White man's way and pushes her back. In the Owl Dance, men join women in a big circle. They interlock arms behind and move to the left, raising up on the toes as they move.

In the Push and Owl dances men and women take turns choosing partners as the district dance leader, the One-who-rules-the-dance, calls for men's or women's choice. An unmarried girl can select for her partner anyone she can marry. She can't take anyone from her own clan because that would be like choosing a brother, and respect behavior meant that we could not touch or hold each other as in a dance. Men could choose unmarried clan sisters of his wife. If my brother-in-law, Barney Old Coyote, was around at one of these dances, he was always my choice for a dance partner, even though I was too young to take part in the dance. When I was a little girl, a *beagatgata*, my mother used to play a joke on me about Barney. She'd say, "He's your 'sister's' husband, and he's your husband, too." I took it seriously, and they all got a kick out of it when I called Barney *"majeda,"* my husband. He'd get quite a kick out of it, too. He was so nice looking and wore a big broad leather belt; I just couldn't help admiring him. It was customary, of course, for Crow men to marry sisters in buffalo-hunting times.

The Push Dance, or Pakaruo, started in Reno District sometime after the First World War, maybe in 1919 or 1920. There were some landless Crees staying with the Crow, and they used to play fiddles and guitars for square dances held in empty houses down Reno way. One Saturday night the Cree musicians didn't show up,

Stylish and handsome Barney Old Coyote, Sr., admired by Agnes during her childhood. Courtesy Hardin Photo Service.

and someone suggested that they get Victor Three Irons, Elmer Takes The Wrinkle, and Howard Shane. They had been to Carlisle and had learned a white man's dance popular at the time, the fox-trot.

Three Irons, Takes The Wrinkle, and Shane brought our own traditional tambourine drums. This was supposed to be a White man's kind of dance, so the singers drummed out our own owl dance songs, but Howard Shane and Elmer Takes The Wrinkle put more swing into the songs. Then the dancers would grab a girl partner and dance White man's style, and they began to do some fancy stepping. The young people were just crazy about it and used to go every weekend, and pretty soon every district was dancing this kind of Push Dance. I always wanted to go but the grown-ups wouldn't take me.

The older people really didn't like the new dance. They were used to the Round or Owl dance, and it was hard to get them to do the Push Dance during our Saturday night socials at the dance lodge. In the thirties, the young people who wanted to dance White-style used to head for secluded spots where they could find an empty house or put up a tent. Here they held a real "pushing around" dance, turning out the lights and hugging and kissing. Besides, in the dark you couldn't tell if your dancing partner was a clan brother or sister, and that's why they put out the lights. After World War II the Push Dance won out over the Owl Dance, and the young people were quite at home in the district dance hall.

At these dances in the district hall there were always a lot of giveaways, small ones. If it was your first dance, you were expected to give something to your clan uncles and aunts. I can remember when they used to ride horses into the dance hall to give to clan uncles. I always hid in my mother's blanket because I was afraid the horse would come our way. There was a dirt floor in the dance hall then, and when they got a board floor, they stopped doing that. Nowadays if someone gives a horse away he will give a bridle instead of a stick as they used to do. If you get a bridle, you know they are going to give you a horse.

Christmas

Dr. Petzoldt, our Baptist missionary, came to us in 1903, and that was the first year we had a Christmas tree and party. In 1903 we also began to go to the Baptist mission school. After that first Christmas, we always had our own Crow celebrations at the time of the Christmas Holy Days and at New Year's. We attended church festivities and then had our own dress-up Christmas dance in our own dance hall. The men's dance societies were very active during the Christmas holiday because that was the time when they recruited new members. There used to be four dance societies, but the main ones today are the Night Hawks and the Big Ear Holes or Rees, named after the Arikara Indians. Donnie's father was a Big Ear Hole member from its beginning, and both Donnie and my father became members. If you had a relative who was a member, you usually were invited to join. New Year's is the time when they adopt, and the Night Hawks and Big Ear Holes bid for new members with money and quilts. They each hold their adoptions, giveaways, and feasting on alternate nights. New members are given special songs and dances.

Like Whites, we Crows like to give the nicest things to relatives and friends at Christmas, but we give more to clan uncles and aunts and to in-laws. Christmas may be the time for a man to give a horse to his brother-in-law, or for his sister or wife to give an elk-tooth dress to a sister-in-law. At home on Christmas Eve we kids put our stockings up and went to bed thinking of the good things we wanted. One time my brother-in-law, John Whiteman, put some dried meat in my stocking. That was all I got because I had misbehaved. I cried when I saw all the good things my brothers and sisters got. I felt bad. Sometimes they put a piece of coal in the stocking of a bad kid.

Our teachers at the Baptist mission school always gave out biblical passages on a slip of paper for each of us to speak. They offered a prize, and because we were shy and quiet in our talking before friends and relatives, they gave their prizes to the boy and girl who recited the loudest. I must have wanted something, for I spoke up real loud one time and got a fine doll. My "brother" Frank Takes The Gun also won a prize for his loud talk.

Teachers also handed out biblical sayings for a Christmas play. We had quite a pageant on Christmas Eve, and I played the part of Mary every time until I got married and moved to Crow Agency. Santa Claus also came on Christmas Eve. They always had two big trees: one for the children and one for grown-ups. The tree for us kids looked pretty with its dolls, little buggies, cars, and balls hanging from its branches; underneath were the packages filled with clothes. While Santa called out our names, we all sat around the tree and then claimed our presents. Boys always got marbles as one of their gifts, and one time my brother Tom received a box that must have held hundreds of marbles. Tom was a good shooter, and he used to win a whole bunch of marbles from the other boys.

Christmas Eve was a time for singing carols, too. Dr.

Petzoldt arranged for the passenger train to stop for fifteen minutes at the Lodge Grass station. While others sang carols, I went through the train and gave out cards decorated with a pine tree to everyone and wished them Merry Christmas. We always walked around Lodge Grass and sang carols. We had great fun sleighing. Pete Lefthand's father, Lefthand, was a fine Christian man, and he used to drop by every Wednesday with his horse-drawn sleigh and take us to the church where a missionary and a teacher lived. He always brought cookies along, and Miss Olds and Miss Johnson wouldn't let us go until we had sung a hymn in Crow for them.

New Year's Dance

The New Year's Dance is a big show-off time, just like the Crow Fair. Men put on their best buckskins and women wear elk-tooth dresses, and everyone makes sure they carry plenty of beadwork. This also is the time when Crows honor young men who have done something good for the Crow people, and their relatives give blankets and other wealth to the clan uncles and aunts of the young men honored. The Long Lodge Dance used to be the main dance at New Year's, but it hasn't been performed for years. Around 1900, Half, Little Owl, and two other Crow men bought the ceremony from some Nez Percé families camped with Crows where the Little Big Horn and Big Horn rivers come together near Hardin. Now the Rees and Night Hawks are the main performers with their adoptions.

The Rees and Night Hawks try to initiate young men who are outstanding and who add color and pageantry to their clubs. Adoptions at New Year's may number from two to eight or ten. The Night Hawks and Rees used to make a parade dance with an American flag, but today they only carry the Crow flag. They have a special song for this parade entrance to which the new recruits dance, and it is a special honor to carry the flag. Usually those honored with the flag have returned from the army or are college graduates.

Today the Rees and Night Hawks number about three hundred members each, but men outnumber women in the Rees, while women outnumber men in the Night Hawks. Members used to give lots of presents to the ones they adopted—blankets, dress goods, scarves, money, and sticks for horses. But they brought in so many members that they don't do that anymore. Usually a clan brother or sister who is a member will act as a sponsor and give a little money.

Men and women volunteer as officers for the year. Women like to serve, and they usually decide what is to be worn at the dance. They may call for a red shirt, or red ribbons over the shirt, and blue jeans or black slacks. A few dancers wear the old-style long winter underwear dyed yellow, red, blue, or black, but Crows started to get away from that after the war.

They used to have a special money dance at New Year's, but now the dancing societies decide whether the man is to pin a couple dollars on his right or left shoulder, or both. The dollar bills are for his female dancing partners. Each man has two women partners, and they dance clockwise as in the owl dance, or they combine a forward and backward step with the circle.

In choosing a partner you go with your in-laws. A man chooses a sister-in-law, like a clan brother's wife or a real brother's wife. Today a man can dance with a clan sister, but in my day that was not so. Crows didn't want you to get familiar with a clan brother or sister then;

oday they don't respect clan rules like they used to.
here is also more marrying by kids who belong to the
ame clan.

Just before twelve o'clock midnight the dancers form
n inner and outer circle. The circles go in opposite
lirections, and people shake hands while drummers
ing the Shake Hands Song. After shaking hands, we
east on special Indian foods that are a part of any New
'ear's celebration.

For this Indian feast each woman brings a pemmican
•all, Indian pudding made of buffalo or other berries,
nd fried bread. In making pemmican we put the dried
neat in the oven and brown it and then pound it up real
ine until it is fluffy. We cook dried chokecherries, drain
ll the water off, and then pound them up. Next we melt
|uite a lot of beef or kidney fat and pour it over the meat
nd the chokecherries before the fat cools. Finally, we
dd a little sugar and salt, mix it all up, and make balls
•ut of it and put them in a cool place. Of course, the
ugar and salt were not a part of the old recipe for
•emmican. My mother told me that they used to take the
:g bones of the buffalo and chop them up with an axe.
'hey boiled the pieces and put the broth aside for the
atty oil to come to the top. They skimmed the fat off like
ream, and that's the fat that makes the best pemmican.
Jowadays we use tallow when we don't have beef or
idney fat. My sister, Amy, mixes a little oleo with the
allow, and her pemmican tastes real good.

Washington's Birthday

:row chiefs and warriors always tried to celebrate Wash-
1gton's Birthday with a parade entrance of the flag and a
var dance. We also had social dances, and usually there

were giveaways. Today basketball tournaments often
conflict with Washington's Birthday, and it is pretty hard
to get a dance organized.

Crows respected Washington as a warrior and as
president, for they had deep respect for their own warriors and chiefs. One time the Crow had a woman who
was an outstanding fighter and leader. She was an Atsina captured when she was a little girl. She could hunt
like a man, and she struck first coup twice and was good
at horse raiding. She had four wives to take care of the
tipi and the hides. They called her Woman Chief. It was
her own Atsina people who killed her in 1854.

When I was growing up, they had a dance called
Woman Chief named after this woman. A Crow man
married to an Atsina woman introduced the dance
around 1902, making use of the Owl Dance and whippers. Whippers came in with the Omaha or Grass Dance
back in the 1870s, and the Hot Dancers of that day took it
up along with the practice of eating dogs.

My sister, Amy, used to go and watch them rehearse
the Woman Chief's dance when she was about five. Four
women carried warbonnets, two owned buggy whips,
and two women chiefs carried a hooked or a lance staff
wrapped with otter. The hooked sticks were like the
ones carried by brave men of the military clubs when we
Crow fought the Piegan, Sioux, Cheyenne, and Arapaho. Two men also belonged to the group and were the
parade leaders. A pipe lighter started the dance with a
smoke-prayer while the drummers drummed out four
songs. When the drummers sang another set of four
songs, the dancers had a parade dance circling the dance
hall. After the parade dance, each of the women asked,
"Who will take care of my stick?" Men volunteered to
make their own parade dance with the stick, warbonnet,

r whip. For that public honor, each had to hold a small
iveaway at the dance hall.

Amy became a whipper when she was just a young girl.
'hey usually adopted young girls to be the switchers. A
lan aunt came and took Amy from her seat and put down
blanket for her to sit on. When they put down a blanket
or you, it meant that they wanted to adopt you. But Amy
lidn't want to be adopted, so she went back to her seat.
'ather told her that she could not do that to a clan aunt;
o Amy went back and sat down on the blanket, while
ather had it announced that he would have the giveaway
he next day. Mother and Dad went the next morning to
uy quilts, blankets, and dress goods. In public it's hard
o refuse an honor, and if you make a fool of yourself, the
Crow are hard on you. They may give you a nickname
hat will never let you forget your mistake.

By her adoption Amy had the right to switch dancers
vho were slow in getting into a war dance. That got the
nen on their feet. They also switched women who didn't
ake part in the Owl Dance, for that was the women's
lance. Sometimes women would come around and take
ome of your beaded stuff if you weren't dancing. And if
ou didn't dance, you wouldn't get it back. This was a
ight the whippers paid for in their adoption. If a switch-
r hurt you, she would make a little giveaway, maybe
iving fifty cents to a clan uncle. At times the father of a
vhipper would have the crier announce that he would
ive a horse to anyone hurt by the whipper. They haven't
ad those whippers at a dance since the twenties. I have
ne of those crooked sticks they danced with. My moth-
r's clan aunt Mary One Goose gave it to me.

During social dances all the chlidren could do was
vatch their favorite dancers and not run around much.
)nce they had a big Round Dance and announced they

wanted just the little ones to dance. I jumped up, and my feet were going so fast that I passed all the other dancers. For being first I had to give a banana to my clan uncles who were present.

Easter

Easter was a big thing for us because we were outfitted with clothes sent to the church by people back East. The clothes came in big barrels and were for both children and adults. The barrels arrived before Easter, and Dr. Petzoldt always had us come to his house to try on the stockings, shoes, ribbons, and dresses. In those days all the girls had long hair, with braids on the sides and one down the back, and he used to put combs in our side braids. With these Easter clothes our parents didn't have to buy anything for us. At church we sang hymns in Crow, took communion, and recited biblical pieces given to us by our teachers. People also celebrated Easter away from church. I remember one time when we had an Easter prayer meeting at Pretty On Top's place. We had colored eggs, and after lunch we went up to the fairgrounds on the bluff above Lodge Grass.

Easter time is important for the Sun Dance, too. When the first thunder sounds in February or March, the pledger sets the time for the first of three "sing" or consecration dances before building the sacred lodge for the Sun Dance in June or July. The districts also have the arrow throw competition after Easter, usually between the middle and end of April.

Sunday Games

People from our district gathered every Sunday to race horses, hold foot races, play the hand game, and watch the women play shinny. The women chose up sides, and whoever lost brought the canned fruit and crackers the next time.

Our missionaries always warned us to stay away from the Sunday Games because of the betting and gambling by the men with elk-tooth counters. The women banged a wooden bowl on the ground to see how the plum-stone dice would turn up. My grandmother played that a lot and for dice took pieces of glass with a design, rounded them off, and marked them. My mother liked to play, too.

The men played "hiding" with elk-tooth counters, and competition between clan champions sometimes reached a fever pitch. Each clan had expert drummer-singers to make medicine for their pointer, and someone always tried to use medicine to make the champion of the other side miss. Clans bet many dollars and even horses. Today "hiding" is a winter competition between districts, and the Crow also have competitions with Oklahoma tribes.

The foot and horse races were exciting. The race course for horses was always long, and I heard that in the 1870s and 1880s they used to hide men along the way who would suddenly appear to scare a horse and rider off the track, sometimes firing a gun real close.

The Sunday gatherings up on the bluff faded during the 1920s. They helped to bring us together. When you live away from each other along the creeks and in the uplands, as the reservation forced us to do, it's hard to keep together. I think we are gradually drifting apart. When we had the fight in the fifties over the Big Horn Canyon dam, it really divided us. We even had two Crow fairs for a couple of years: one at Lodge Grass for the Mountain Crow bunch, and one at Crow Agency for the River Crows.

In the old days the Mountain and the River Crow bands provided the main identity for the people, outside of the tribe. Now it is the district that is important in politics and competitions. Members of the Stout or Big-lodge and Newly-made-lodge clans were the most numerous, and most of them settled around Lodge Grass. So did most of the chiefs. It's the same today, and the Big-lodge has more educated young people than any other clan. We are good competitors, and there is a saying, "All nations unite against Lodge Grass." Lodge Grass comes out on top most of the time and has held the arrow-throwing crown for eleven years. Also, when they put on a Sun Dance, Lodge Grass dancers always exceed one hundred. We celebrate our victories in our district song: "Lodge Grass District is a good home, and if you want to celebrate a victory dance, live there!"

The first name for Lodge Grass District was Chiefs' Creek, because in the old days the Crow bands frequently met where Greasy Creek (Lodge Grass Creek) and the Little Big Horn River come together. Then people began calling us Eshebea or Muddy Mouths. In 1946 our district crier, Jack Covers Up, told the people at the arrow throw camp at Pryor that we wanted to be called by our original name, Chiefs' Creek, but everyone still calls us Muddy Mouths.

Arrow Throw

An arrow throw was held at Pryor in April of 1946 to celebrate the return of our soldier boys from the war. This was an important event for the Crow; just about everybody was there, and the tents and tipis made a big camp. All the districts fielded teams, and six of our clans (Whistling-water, Tied-in-a-knot, Piegan, Greasy-inside-the-mouth, Big-lodge, Newly-made-lodge) competed against each other, too. Whenever the districts competed, as they did at Pryor, you could count on a hand game in the evening.

In the arrow throw, players throw iron-tipped arrows for a distance of forty to fifty yards. Each district team has three players. They throw out a target arrow, and players try to lean their arrows against it. If the feathers touch, that earns four points, and shaft to shaft gives three. Players try to trick each other by throwing the target arrow a longer or shorter distance, or more upright or slanting, as they size up their opponents. There is a lot of betting, and each team puts up a purse. The team that wins the first throw gets a part of the purse, and that was $30 in 1946. To win, the district team must be the first to get fifty points. On the second day at Pryor, the pot for the winners amounted to $450. With six teams, if you put in a dollar and won, you got six back.

Old Runs In The Bunch from Pryor started the game with a war story, which was relayed by the district crier, Oliver Lion Shows:

I was on a war party and got into enemy territory and captured some horses from the enemy. I brought these horses to my people; and I gave them to my brother-in-law, my brothers, father-in-law, and sisters-in-law. What I did on that day was pretty good in getting those horses and bringing them back. So I wish for my team to win and for the money to be distributed among the Pryor people.

He then threw the target arrow only about twenty feet, which brought some good laughs.

As the host district, Pryor's team leader started the game by throwing the target arrow the regulation dis-

tance, and the Black-lodges from Crow Agency came the
closest and won $30 for their district. Every time a
district player made a good strike, a clan uncle sang his
praise song and told what a fine player he was, and then
the clan uncle sang his praise song again. Every time a
district reached ten points toward the fifty, the game
stopped while a veteran recited a war deed and wished
luck to his team. There were more than twenty-two
stops for these good-luck stories. At one point, Charlie
Ten Bear, the crier from the Black-lodges, told Francis
Lincoln's story: "The Short or Wolf People took an island
away from us and then we went over and took it back.
And the Old-Man-Up-There in heaven looked down
upon us in that action. That's the truth, and I hope this
team of mine wins in a hurry to make this fifty points."
With that he called upon his clan uncles, who were from
the Tied-in-a-knot clan, to come and get some blankets,
quilts, and money he was giving out. This gave the Tied-
in-a-knot clan uncles and aunts the right to sing their
clan praise song: "We own the chief of all the chiefs."

When Big Horn District reached a ten-point mark,
their crier, Bird Horse, announced that one of their veterans, Big Bird, had been in the South Pacific with the
Forty-Third Division. He had killed many of the Wolf
People and in one case had shot one pretty close in the
chest. He wished his true luck for his people to win. To
Blake Whiteman, a clan uncle who had given him his
name, Big Bird gave a horse. Blake walked in a circle
sunwise, leading the horse and singing his praise song:
"There's gladness in my heart. I feel like smiling!"

Earlier, when the Big Horn team reached a ten-point
mark, Bird Horse announced they had no veterans at
hand because the veterans were off drinking. So they
brought Crooked Arm on to tell about his running suc-

cesses: "I was one time the champion foot racer of the Crow Reservation. I think that is a great thing to be first among my people. What I said is the truth, and on that truth I hope we win this game." Crooked Arm had Bird Horse also announce that he had a stud horse worth $200 and he was giving it to his clan uncles to sell and divide the money.

Goes Ahead of Pryor used this big public gathering to honor his two sons, Carter and Vincent, with giveaways. He also had giveaways for his stepson, Charlie De-Crane, and his son-in-law, Posy Whiteman. As it turned out, this arrow throw was won by Pryor, and Carter Goes Ahead was second in individual scoring behind Buster of Wyola. Our Lodge Grass thrower, Moses Old Bull, came in third. Carter had the nickname of "Cardy."

In celebration of the big victory over the Iron Hats and the Short People, clan uncles gave their honor names to many of their veteran "children." Goes Ahead bought Plentyhawk's name for Vincent, who had been overseas. The drummer-singers learned a new song for the giveaway:

They name this boy after Plentyhawk.
Plentyhawk, you gave yourself away [that is, went off to war].
That is a very honorable deed that you did.
You are not afraid of the enemy!

Besides the usual blankets, quilts, dress goods, and scarves, Goes Ahead gave a warbonnet to Plays and one to Tits, clan uncles of Carter and Vincent. Giving a warbonnet was the highest honor in a giveaway, both for the one who received it and the one who gave it. Then the Bad-war-honors and Whistling-water clan uncles and aunts had the right to sing their clan and individual praise songs. Posy Whiteman's clan uncle, Robert Half, also received a warbonnet, and the Big-lodges broke out their praise songs for their "child," Posy. The drummer-singers, including the women singers for the war dance honoring Vincent and Carter, were all from the Big-lodge and Newly-made-lodge clans. They drummed the war dance four times while Vincent and Posy danced, but Carter was bashful and skipped out. He was in the army but had not gone overseas and was back on furlough. Vincent had been in the fighting and was discharged. Goes Ahead had to make excuses for Carter, since he could not get him to return.

This was the seventh giveaway by Goes Ahead for his boys. He really wanted his boys to get ahead and was a fine Crow father. Blake Whiteman, a clan uncle to Vincent and Carter, spoke out in praise of Goes Ahead: "I have been looking on all the districts. I have seen that Goes Ahead is doing a good job in raising his boys; and I wish all the Crows would do the same in good conduct."

In the feast which went with the giveaway, Goes Ahead and his wife's Sore-lip clan relatives must have fed at least three hundred people. Each person furnished his own eating utensils, and small boys and girls came running with granite or enameled plates, small bowls, cups, knives, forks, and spoons for clan uncles and aunts, fathers, and grandparents. Cold pork and beans, fried or boiled beef, fried sweet bread, white store bread, jelly rolls, cookies, doughnuts, cinnamon buns, canned mixed fruits, and strongly sweetened coffee were laid out on tables. You don't see that sugary-sweet coffee anymore.

Men of the Newly-made-lodge clan headed the food line, followed by the Big-lodges, Whistling-waters, and then anyone. The Newly-made-lodges took the lead because they were the clan uncles and aunts of Vincent and Carter and the feast was for them. The Big-lodges were next in line because they were close partners of the Newly-made-lodges. The Whistling-waters were there because they were clan uncles and aunts of Posy Whiteman, who was a brother-in-law of Vincent and Carter. Women lined up behind the men without regard to their clans, but so long as a line of men remained, latecomers crowded ahead of the women. Among the Crow, men always lead women when walking, talking, and eating and in the distribution of goods at giveaways. Men are always first, although that custom is beginning to break down.

The win by Pryor didn't end our good time. They set up another seven-point game for a distance throw of sixty yards, with a purse of $50 for each district. Lodge Grass luck wasn't good, and Pryor won, collecting $150 from the rest of us. Then they set up a clan game for six points and a purse of $25. The Whistling-waters, Tied-in-a-knots, Greasy-inside-the-mouths, Big-lodges, and Newly-made-lodges were beaten by the Piegans. Our Whistling-water team got only one point. The Tied-in-a-knot clan was not ready to give up in the competition and challenged all the other clans to a game of hiding.

We had great fun at this arrow throw. In camp we got to see our relatives from other districts, and there was plenty of good food and good times. One of our Hidatsa relatives was visiting, and he was so happy with Carter Goes Ahead's play that he gave him his name, Walking Soldier. This Hidatsa had been in World War I, and he reported that the man from the old days who had given him that name was still living. When he got back to his people, he was going to tell them as well as the old man what an outstanding player Carter was, winning the long-distance throw and winning for his clan. For Carter to carry the name of Walking Soldier was a thing of great pride for the Hidatsa, and he was going to give Carter a praise song when he returned. But the Crow wanted him to sing the praise song right then, which he did. Then Carter's clan relatives had to give him some quilts, money, and other things to pay for that song right then. Some clan uncles gave away all their ceremonial honor names to their soldier "children." Bear Ground gave away all of his, so he paid Simpson Sings Pretty a horse for the name of the Crow Chief Sits In The Middle Of The Ground. He had the crier announce that this was the name he wanted to be called by in the future. Old people are always looking for ways to help their clan children.

In the Crow way, if you want to be an arrow thrower, a guesser in the game of hiding, or a public herald, you need to acquire the medicine-right from a qualified person. In the old buffalo days chiefs were qualified to lead the Crow if they had medicine that would bring luck and plenty to eat to the people. It's the same way today with arrow throwers, hand game guessers, or anyone who acts for the people or prays for them. You need someone with good luck to lead you.

Memorial Day

Crows respect those who have passed away by decorating their graves with flowers on Memorial Day. Churches hold special services, and Lodge Grass families go to the graves located on the western bluff above the Little Big Horn River. Even today we don't like to say the person's name, for you might call him back. Some leave artificial flowers on the grave, and at the cemetery on Memorial Day, you will always see someone who is showing respect by crying out that he has lost a brother, a father, or a mother.

The cemetery was something new for us on the reservation. In the old days people wrapped their loved ones in a buffalo hide that had been part of the tipi cover. They put the body on a four-legged platform, or in a tree, or slipped it into a rock crevice along the way of their travel. People continued to bury the dead on platforms and in trees when they first came to the reservation.

We have always been afraid of ghosts. When someone passed away in a tipi or in a log house on the reservation, the Crow never took him out through the regular door but out a window. They wanted the ghost to go to the Other Side People right away for fear the ghost might stay around and take another person with them. They took the dead person out immediately after death, and if they knew someone was real sick or might die, they put him in a little tent away from the house. Now people often die in the hospital, and from there the Crow take the body to the funeral home.

It was the custom to enclose personal belongings with the body. A man would take his bow, knife, and medicine to the grave if he hadn't passed them on to his son. When a woman passed away, clan sisters usually took the tipi poles and other domestic things, and near relatives still do that today, picking up dishes, chairs, and pictures. Reservation life brought us new kinds of household pots and appliances, and I have seen sewing machines and frying pans left at the grave.

Fourth of July

On the Fourth of July in the old days, Crows from all the districts came and camped on the bluff above Lodge Grass. Families put up tipis, and each district camped together. Everyone moved on horseback and in wagons.

There was always a parade with people showing off their new horses and buggies and everyone dressed in his best Indian outfit.

Criers from the different districts got everybody up early. They told us to take a bath and to dress in our best outfits. The men always dressed with their war honors and carried their medicines in a sham battle. If someone from a different tribe was visiting, they brought him out for the sham battle. The old warriors collected their grandchildren and watched to see who would be the first to strike coup on the enemy visitors. The clan uncle would take the first coup striker around the camp, singing a praise song, while the coup striker's relatives hurried to collect things for the giveaway. They gave to the visiting enemy, too. Sometimes they had the women dance the Shoshoni Dance to honor a warrior. They put on their best clothes, some wearing reservation hats, and the warrior and the women charged and retreated as in a fight with the enemy.

Grandma Stays By The Water always took us grandkids to the Muddy Mouth campground in the flat below the bluff. Ben Pease always had a stand there, and you could buy hamburgers, pop, candy, chewing gum, and sometimes firecrackers. The boys always threw lighted firecrackers at us girls, which made us bunch together in fright, especially when they threw the firecrackers at our feet.

Later in the afternoon they had horse races. In the relay races they had four to six riders. Horses for each rider were stationed around the track. A rider had to take his saddle from the horse he was riding and put it on the waiting horse. Whoever came in first was the winner, and it got exciting when a rider would go skidding off his horse because he hadn't tightened the cinch enough. Francis Leforge won every time. Sometimes Barney Old Coyote would have them tie a rope across the racetrack and he walked that rope, balancing himself without a pole. There were always exhibits under the grandstand, usually garden stuff and sewing, the same as at the Crow Fair.

They don't have those foot, horse, and relay races any more at the Fourth of July celebrations. We get that kind of excitement now at our rodeo. Each district celebrates the Fourth of July with its own feast and dances in the local hall, arranged by a volunteer recreation commit- tee. The old tribal get-togethers on the Fourth of July went out with the horse and buggy.

Summer Camps

Every June we Baptists went to a church camp for a week or two to be with other religious people. Sometimes we went to Pryor, at other times to the Wolf Mountains. We looked forward to the camp, and someone always an- nounced it by saying, "They are going to the camp to pray."

Looking back, it seems like all they did was to have prayers from sunrise to the time they went to bed. As in the buffalo-hunting days, the old people went into the higher hills to pray. Some always stayed behind to make breakfast. Throughout the day older persons prayed in Crow, and our fathers and mothers wouldn't let us play because they didn't want us to disturb people in their prayers.

Our Baptist missionaries usually brought religious leaders from other tribes, but the one I liked best was a Crow man from Pryor, John Frost. He was a strong Christian and had so much faith that tears would run. During a meeting everyone took part in giving testimony. They still have camp meetings, but these are changed, and everything is in English.

The Sun Dance

By June people are looking forward to the Sun Dance, and after that the Crow Fair and Rodeo. The Sun Dance draws a lot of people from all districts, but the local district people are the real organizers and providers. Big Lodge is another name for the Sun Dance today, but in the old days they called it making a little tipi, imitative of the Sun's medicine tipi.

A pledger and his near relatives and close friends take care of the costs of bringing a big cottonwood tree with forked branches as the center pole, twelve pines about forty feet in length, as well as twelve uprights and twelve stringers, and the brush cover. They get volunteers, mostly brothers-in-law, clan brothers, and friends; even so, it is very costly, for the pledger has to put on a big feast at the end. He usually gives something to the head drummer for his smoke-prayer and to the veteran who marks the three black rings around the tree and wishes good luck for all. He must give a little present to the veteran selected to build the sacred fire in the lodge and to keep it going, and then there is payment to the medicine man who directs the ceremony. Building the dance lodge takes all day, and the dancers go in after the sun goes down and a full moon is coming up in the east.

The Big Lodge ceremony is not the old Crow Sun Dance. William Big Day of Pryor brought the Shoshoni Sun Dance to the Crow in 1941 with the aid of the Shoshoni medicine man John Trehero. In the traditional Crow ceremony a man in mourning pledged a Sun Dance to get revenge on the enemy. Today they dance mostly because of sickness or to change their luck. The dancers suffer without food or water for two and a half days, running at the buffalo head attached to the center tree and dancing back to their places. While dancing, they blow their prayers through an eagle-bone whistle to the Creator, or to Grandfather Sun, according to their belief. They also offer tobacco in a smoke-prayer at the tree. If the buffalo on the center tree knocks a dancer down, he expects to get a gift of power, perhaps a power to cure.

A medicine man cures people by drawing power given by the Creator from the forked center tree. He takes bad stuff out of a person with his medicine feathers and throws it away to the east or to the Four Winds. Some medicine men can draw water from the tree to cool the weary dancers and keep them going. Crows say that if your soul during a dream goes to where there is a spring and drinks from it, you will never feel that burning in your throat for the rest of the dance. Dancing then will be easy, and you will feel as if you are flying as you run at the buffalo and pray. Dancers are barefoot, and the paths they make to the buffalo look like the spokes of a wheel. The area west of the tree is sacred, and everyone must go there barefoot to be doctored.

A lodge pole that runs from the west edge directly east is known as the Chief's Pole. It is forked with two green tips, and they put an eagle there as in a nest. The eagle is Grandfather Sun's messenger, and the pledger and medicine man share this pole in sending prayers and receiving messages from Sun. The main power comes from the Creator, the one the Crow call Akbatatdea, The Maker Of Everything.

The second day is the hardest, and relatives bring sweet-smelling sage and cattails for the dancers' beds. A brother, clan brother, or brother-in-law is always ready to put up two poles at the foot of a dancer's bed that he can hold on to when tired. It is the same for those who bring cattails or donate the blue flags and white flags and the Bull Durham tobacco offerings placed on the forks of the center tree. Everyone tries to help the dancers who are sacrificing themselves in this prayer way to change their luck and to help a loved one get through a sickness. On this second day the dancers feel the dryness of their throats, and the suffering without food and water under the hot sun makes them very tired. But they dance hard and pray with sincerity so they will be blessed. Most people like to be doctored on the second day, for the medicine man can draw strong power from the tree for their cures.

Every morning at sunrise the dancers line up to greet Grandfather Sun. The power is close now, and the dancers pray to be free from their aches and pains, and they pray for those who are dear to them. The pledger gives a special prayer as Sun casts his powers over the sacred fire. An elder first clears the way of all evil with a cedar prayer, and then the pledger can offer his tobacco prayer. He prays for the dancers and their wishes, for the sick, and that the old people may live longer. He asks that children grow up healthy and that his own wishes be granted. He also prays for the government and people of the United States: "This is our homeland, and we don't want any stranger to come and take it over."

The Sun Dance ends on the morning of the third day when the dancers take water brought by a virtuous woman and blessed by respected old men. No dancer leaves until he has asked a clan uncle or aunt to pray for him, and of course he gives the clan uncle a quilt or blanket and perhaps some money.

They used the Sun Dance a lot during the war to bring our Crow boys safely home, and we lost only two of our boys. During the war a few old men and women fasted, and some men pledged to dance or to fast in every Sun Dance until the war was over. That might mean sacrificing themselves in three or four Sun Dances a year.

The Sun Dance changed during the fifties, and women made the biggest change when they danced and prayed with eagle-bone whistles just like the men. They saw Shoshoni women in Idaho dancing in the Sun Dance. Today there are almost as many women dancers as men. In the lodge, men and women dancers are kept separate. Men take their places to the west of the center tree, the more sacred ground of the lodge and from which it is easier to see and to run at the buffalo. If there are so many dancers that they fill the lodge, then the whole lodge becomes sacred ground. That happened in Lodge Grass in 1975.

Men and women are separated in the lodge because in Crow belief "medicine fathers" with sacred power to give do not like to be around women who are having a menstrual flow. To make sure that there is no interference with the sacred power, any woman having her period is required to leave the dance lodge, whether a dancer or an onlooker. This applies only to Indian women, for this way of praying was given to Indians and not to White people.

Early in July, after the Sun Dances, people get their tipi poles ready for our grand tribal camp, the Crow Fair. We all look ahead to that time with great joy because it is the beginning of new happiness and of new luck and blessings for us during the year. We can relax with relatives, friends, and visiting tribal members. We can be ourselves—be Indians.

Bibliography

Ahler, Stanley A., Thomas D. Thiessen, and Michael K. Trimble. 1991. *People of the Willows: The Prehistory and Early History of the Hidatsa Indians.* Fargo: University of North Dakota Press.

Bowers, Alfred W. 1965. *Hidatsa Social and Ceremonial Organization.* Smithsonian Institution, Bureau of American Ethnology Bulletin 194. Washington, D.C.

Bradley, C. C., Jr. 1972. *After the Buffalo Days.* Crow Agency, Montana: Crow Central Education Commission.

Bradley, James H. 1896–1923. "The Bradley Manuscript in the Montana Historical Society Library." Montana Historical Society Collections, vols. 2–3, 8–9. Helena, Montana.

Bureau of Indian Affairs. 1968. *Crow Cattle Ranching Operations.* U.S. Department of the Interior, Report No. 187. Billings, Montana.

Bureau of Indian Affairs. 1975. *Draft Programmatic Environmental Statement, DES-75-2: Projected Coal Development, Crow Indian Reservation.* Billings, Montana: U.S. Department of the Interior.

Campbell, William S. 1927. "The Tipis of the Crow Indians." *American Anthropologist* 29:87–104.

Catlin, George. 1973. *Letters and Notes on the Manners, Customs, and Conditions of the North American Indians.* 2 vols. New York: Dover Publications, Inc.

Clark, William P. 1982. *The Indian Sign Language.* Reprint,

Lincoln: University of Nebraska Press Bison Book. Original, 1885.

Culbertson, Thaddeus. 1952. *Journal of an Expedition to the Mauvaises Terres and the Upper Missouri in 1850.* Edited by John F. McDermott. Smithsonian Institution, Bureau of American Ethnology Bulletin 147. Washington, D.C.

Curtis, Edward S. 1970. "The Apsaroke, or Crows." In *The North American Indian.* 20 vols. 4:3–126, 175–80, 197–210. Reprint, New York: Johnson Reprint Corporation. Original, 1909.

———. 1970. "The Hidatsa." In *The North American Indian.* 20 vols. 4:129–72, 180–96, 210–11. Reprint, New York: Johnson Reprint Corporation. Original, 1909.

Denig, Edwin T. 1930. "Indian Tribes of the Upper Missouri, the Assiniboin." In *Forty-Sixth Annual Report,* edited by J.N.B. Hewitt, 395–628. Washington, D.C.: Smithsonian Institution, Bureau of American Ethnology.

———. 1985. *Five Indian Tribes of the Upper Missouri* (Sioux, Arickaras, Assiniboines, Crees, Crows). Edited by John C. Ewers. Norman: University of Oklahoma Press.

Ehrlich, Clara. 1937. "Tribal Culture in Crow Mythology." *Journal of American Folk-Lore* 50:307–408.

Ewers, John C. 1968. "The Indian Trade of the Upper Missouri Before Lewis and Clark." In J. C. Ewers, *Indian Life on the Upper Missouri,* 14–33. Norman: University of Oklahoma Press.

Feder, Norman. 1959. "The Crow Indians of Montana." *American Indian Hobbyist* 5 (5 and 6).

———. 1980. "Crow Blanket Strip Rosettes." *American Indian Art* 6(1):41–45.

Frey, Rodney. 1987. *The World of the Crow Indians.* Norman: University of Oklahoma Press.

Frison, George C. 1979. "The Crow Indian Occupation of the High Plains: The Archaeological Evidence." *Archaeology in Montana* 20(3):3–16.

Galante, Gary. 1980. "Crow Lance Cases or Sword Scabbards." *American Indian Art* 6(1):64–73.

Harcey, Dennis W., and Brian R. Croone, with Joe Medicine Crow. 1993. *White-Man-Runs-Him*. (Crow Scout with Custer.) Evanston, Illinois: Evanston Publishing, Inc.

Hayden, Ferdinand V. 1862. "Contributions to the Ethnography and Philology of the Indian Tribes of the Missouri Valley." American Philosophical Society, *Transactions* 12(2):234–461.

Heidenreich, C. Adrian. 1979. "The Bearing of Ethnohistoric Data on the Crow-Hidatsa Separation(s)." *Archaeology in Montana* 20(3):54–67.

Hoxie, Frederick E. 1984. "Building a Future on the Past: Crow Indian Leadership in an Era of Division and Reunion." In *Indian Leadership*, edited by Walter L. Williams, 76–84. Manhattan, Kansas: Sunflower University Press.

Hultkrantz, Ake. 1953. *Conceptions of the Soul Among North American Indians: A Study of Religious Ethnology*. The Ethnographical Museum of Sweden, Monograph Series, Publication No. 1. Stockholm.

Jackson, Donald J., editor. 1962. *Letters of the Lewis and Clark Expedition, with Related Documents 1783–1854*. Urbana: University of Illinois Press.

Kammen, Robert, Joe Marshall, and Frederick Lefthand. 1992. *Soldiers Falling into Camp: The Battles at the Rosebud and the Little Big Horn*. Encampment, Wyoming: Affiliated Writers of America.

Kappler, Charles J. 1972. *Indian Treaties, 1778–1883*. New York: Interland Publishing Company.

Kaschube, Dorothea. 1967. *Structural Elements of the Language of the Crow Indians of Montana*. University of Colorado Studies, Series in Anthropology No. 14. Boulder.

Kiste, Robert. N.d. "Crow Peyotism." Manuscript.

Koch, Ronald P. 1977. *Dress Clothing of the Plains Indians*. Norman: University of Oklahoma Press.

Kurz, Rudolph Friederich. 1937. *Journal of Rudolph Friederich Kurz*. Edited by J.N.B. Hewitt, translated by Myrtis

Jarrell. Smithsonian Institution, Bureau of American Ethnology, Bulletin 115. Washington, D.C.

Lanford, Benson. 1980. "Parfleche and Crow Beadwork Designs." *American Indian Art* 6(1):32–39.

Larocque, François-Antoine. 1985. "François-Antoine Larocque's 'Yellowstone Journal.'" In *Early Fur Trade on the Northern Plains: Canadian Traders Among the Mandan and Hidatsa Indians, 1738–1818,* edited by W. Raymond Wood and Thomas D. Thiessen, 156–220. Norman: University of Oklahoma Press.

La Vérendrye, P. G. de Varennes. 1927. *Journals and Letters of Pierre Gaulter de Vérendrye and His Sons.* Edited by L. J. Burpee. Toronto: Champlain Society Publication.

Leonard, Zenas. 1904. *Adventures of Zenas Leonard, Fur Trader and Trapper, 1831–1836.* Edited by W. F. Wagner. Cleveland: Burrows Brothers Company.

Lessard, F. Fennis. 1980. "Crow Indian Art: The Nez Perce Connection." *American Indian Art* 6(1):54–63.

Linderman, Frank B. 1931. *Old Man Coyote (Crow).* New York: The Junior Literary Guild.

———. 1962. *Plenty Coups, Chief of the Crows.* Reprint, Lincoln: University of Nebraska Press Bison Book. Original, 1930.

———. 1972. *Pretty Shield, Medicine Woman of the Crows.* Reprint, Lincoln: University of Nebraska Press Bison Book. Original, 1932.

Loeb, Barbara. 1980. "Mirror Bags and Bandoleer Bags: A Comparison." *American Indian Art* 6(1):46–53, 88.

Lowie, Robert H. 1912. "Social Life of the Crow Indians." American Museum of Natural History, *Anthropological Papers* 9:179–248.

———. 1913. "Societies of the Crow, Hidatsa, and Mandan Indians." American Museum of Natural History, *Anthropological Papers* 11:219–358.

———. 1913. "Military Societies of the Crow Indians." American Museum of Natural History, *Anthropological Papers* 11:145–217.

———. 1915. "The Sun Dance of the Crow Indians." American Museum of Natural History, *Anthropological Papers* 16:1–50.

———. 1916. "Plains Indian Age-Societies." American Museum of Natural History, *Anthropological Papers* 11:877–992.

———. 1917. "Notes on the Social Organization and Customs of the Mandan, Hidatsa, and Crow Indians." American Museum of Natural History, *Anthropological Papers* 21:3–99.

———. 1918. "Myths and Traditions of the Crow Indians." American Museum of Natural History, *Anthropological Papers* 25:1–308.

———. 1919. "The Tobacco Society of the Crow Indians." American Museum of Natural History, *Anthropological Papers* 21:103–200.

———. 1922. "The Material Culture of the Crow Indians." American Museum of Natural History, *Anthropological Papers* 21:203–70.

———. 1922. "Crow Indian Art." American Museum of Natural History, *Anthropological Papers* 21:271–322.

———. 1922. "The Religion of the Crow Indians." American Museum of Natural History, *Anthropological Papers* 25:311–444.

———. 1924. "Minor Ceremonies of the Crow Indians." American Museum of Natural History, *Anthropological Papers* 21:325–65.

———. 1935. *The Crow Indians.* New York: Farrar and Rinehart.

———. 1941. "The Crow Language: Grammatical Sketch and Analyzed Text." University of California Publications in American Archaeology and Ethnology, 39:1–142. Berkeley.

Marquis, Thomas B. 1974. *Memoirs of a White Crow Indian (Thomas H. Leforge).* Lincoln: University of Nebraska Press Bison Book.

Maximilian, Prince of Wied. 1966. "Travels in the Interior of North America, 1832–1835." In *Early Western Travels,*

1748–1846, edited by Reuben Gold Thwaites, 22:346–55. New York: AMS Press, Inc.

Medicine Crow, Joe. 1939. "The Effects of European Culture Contacts upon the Economic, Social, and Religious Life of Crow Indians." Master's thesis, University of Southern California, Los Angeles.

———. 1979a. "The Crow Migration Story." *Archaeology in Montana* 20(3):63–72.

———. 1979b. *Medicine Crow.* Crow Agency, Montana: Crow Central Education Commission.

———. 1992. *From the Heart of the Crow Country.* New York: Orion Books.

Medicine Crow, Joe, and Charles Bradley, Jr. 1976. *The Crow Indians: 100 Years of Acculturation.* Wyola, Montana: Wyola Bilingual Project.

Medicine Crow, Joe, and Daniel Press. 1966. *A Handbook of Crow Indian Laws and Treaties.* Crow Agency, Montana.

Medicine Horse, Mary Helen. *A Dictionary of Everyday Crow.* Crow Agency: Bilingual Materials Development Center.

Morgan, Lewis Henry. 1959. *The Indian Journals, 1859–62.* Edited by Leslie A. White. Ann Arbor: The University of Michigan Press.

Murdock, George P. 1934. "The Crow Indians of the Western Plains." In *Our Primitive Contemporaries,* 264–90. New York: The MacMillan Company.

Nabokov, Peter, editor. 1970. *Two Leggings: The Making of a Crow Warrior* [manuscript of William Wildschut]. New York: Thomas Y. Crowell Apollo Edition.

Old Coyote, Henry. 1974. *Crow Indian Child Raising.* Crow Agency, Montana: Crow Agency Bilingual Education.

Old Coyote, Mickey. 1988. *Apsaaloka—Then and Now.* Crow Agency, Montana. Bilingual Materials Development Center.

Old Horn, Dale. 1986. Baaanniile. Crow Agency, Montana: Bilingual Materials Development Center.

Ostwalt, Wendell H. 1978. "The Crow: Plains Warrors and Bison Hunters." In *This Land Was Theirs: A Study of*

North American Indians, 257–95. 3d ed. New York, Wiley.

Pease, Eloise Whitebear, editor. 1968. *Absaraka.* (Crow Tribal Treaty Centennial Issue.) Billings, Montana.

Pease, Eloise, Adrienne Johnson, Torrey Johnson, and Richard Fox, Jr. 1976. *Grass, Tipis, and Black Gold.* Billings, Montana: Artecraft.

Prucha, Francis Paul, editor. 1990. *Documents of United States Indian Policy.* 2d ed. Lincoln: University of Nebraska Press.

Simms, S. C. 1903. *Traditions of the Crows.* Field Columbian Museum, Publication 85, Anthropological Series, Vol. 2, No. 6. Chicago.

––––––. 1904. "Cultivation of Medicine Tobacco by the Crows." *American Anthropologist* 6:331–35.

Stewart, Omer C. 1987. *Peyote Religion: A History.* Norman: University of Oklahoma Press.

Taylor, Colin. 1981. "Crow Rendezvous." *American Indian Studies Series,* No. 1, 1–37. London: Early Westerners Society.

Trenholm, Virginia C., and Maurine Carley. 1964. *The Shoshonis: Sentinels of the Rockies.* Norman: University of Oklahoma Press.

Voget, Fred W. 1964. "Warfare and the Integration of Crow Indian Culture." In *Explorations in Cultural Anthropology: Essays in Honor of George Peter Murdock,* edited by Ward B. Goodenough, 483–509. New York: McGraw Hill Book Company.

––––––. 1980. "Tradition, Identity, and Adaptive Change Among the Crow of Montana." In *Political Organization of Native North Americans,* edited by Ernest L. Schusky, 163–87. Washington, D.C.: University Press of America, Inc.

––––––. 1984. *The Shoshoni-Crow Sun Dance.* Norman: University of Oklahoma Press.

––––––. 1987. "The Crow Indian Give-Away, a Primary Instrument for Cultural Adaptation and Persistence." *Anthropos* 82:207–16.

———. 1990. "Crow." Manuscript, in press.

Wagner, Glendolin D., and William A. Allen. 1987. *Blankets and Moccasins: Plenty Coups and His People, the Crows.* Lincoln: University of Nebraska Press Bison Book.

Weist, Katherine M. 1977. "An Ethnohistorical Analysis of Crow Political Alliances." *The Western Canadian Journal of Anthropology* 7(4):34–54.

Wildschut, William. 1975. *Crow Indian Medicine Bundles.* Edited by John C. Ewers. Contributions from the Museum of the American Indian, Heye Foundation, Vol. 17. New York: Heye Foundation.

Wildschut, William, and John E. Ewers. 1959. "Crow Indian Beadwork: A Descriptive and Historical Study." Contributions from the Museum of the American Indian, Heye Foundation, Vol. 16, 1–55. New York: Heye Foundation.

Wood, W. Raymond. 1980. "Plains Trade in Prehistoric and Protohistoric Intertribal Relations." In *Anthropology on the Great Plains,* edited by W. Raymond Wood and Margot Liberty, 98–109. Lincoln: University of Nebraska Press.

———. 1986. *The Origins of the Hidatsa Indians: A Review of Ethnohistorical and Traditional Data.* With a chapter of Jeffery R. Hanson. Reprints in Anthropology, Vol. 32. Reprint, Lincoln, Nebraska: J&L Reprint Company. Original, 1980.

Wood, W. Raymond, and Alan S. Downer. 1977. "Notes on the Crow-Hidatsa Schism." *Plains Anthropologist, Memoir* 13:83–100.

Wood, W. Raymond, and Margot Liberty, editors. 1980. *Anthropology on the Great Plains.* Lincoln: University of Nebraska Press.

Wood, W. Raymond, and Thomas D. Thiessen, editors. 1985. *Early Fur Trade on the Northern Plains: Canadian Traders Among the Mandan and Hidatsa Indians, 1738–1818.* Norman: University of Oklahoma Press.

Yellowtail, Robert Summers, Sr. 1973. *Robert Summers Yellow-*

tail Sr. Albuquerque: Cold Type Service of New Mexico.
Yellowtail, Thomas. 1991. *Yellowtail: Crow Medicine Man and Sun Dance Chief, an Autobiography.* Edited by Michael Oren Fitzgerald. Norman: University of Oklahoma Press.

Index

Laubin, Reginald, 136
Little Coyote. *See* Creation

Makpay, sacred essence, 6–7
Marriage, 49–50, 53, 61
Maternal uncle. *See* Kinship
Medicine: adoption, 10; bundle,
   12–13, 30; dreams, 18–19, 20,
   40; "father"-"son," 9–10, 12;
   man, 59, 199; necklace, 40–
   41; painting, 12; pipe, 20;
   pipe association, 13; powers,
   12; quest, 11–12; rocks, 12,
   19; song, 12; transfer, 10
Miss Indian America, 135–36
Money: dance, 182; tree, 29
Moon: full, 13; new, 111; spirit
   being, 11
Morning Star, 23. *See also* Old
   Woman's Grandchild
Mother Earth, 18
Mountain Crow, band, 168–69
Mourning, 16, 165–67

Names, 41–42, 65–66, 193–94
National Indian Congress, 140
Newly-made-lodge, clan, 197
No Vitals (Crow chief), 14–15

Old Coyote, Barney, Sr., 177
Old Man Coyote, 7–8, 85–86.
   See Creation
Old Man Up There, 190
Old Woman's Grandchild, 11,
   14, 16, 23. *See* Morning Star
Omens, owls, 81–82
"Other Mother," mother's sister,
   87, 88, 90–91
Other Side Camp (people), 8,
   195

Payment, four traditional gifts,
   39
Pease, Bill, 136
Pease, Ferale, 105, 145–49
Pentecostal, church, 32
Petzoldt, Dr. (Baptist mission-
   ary), 47–48, 130, 151, 179, 186
Peyote, 30
Piegan: Blackfeet band, 61;
   Crow clan, 193
Pipeholder, war chief, 20. *See
   also* medicine, pipe
Pipelighter, 20
Praise song, 117, 190, 194
Prayer, 7, 57–58, 74–78
Pregnancy, beliefs and pro-
   cedures, 35–38, 42–43
Pryor, district and village, 27
Punishment, children, 84–85

Religion, monotheism, 7. *See also*
   Crow Indian historic culture
Reservation. *See* Crow Indian
   reservation culture
Ritual numbers, 23
River Crow, band, 4, 168–69
Rock medicines, 19

Seasonal migration, buffalo
   hunting, 168–69
Seven Bulls (brothers), star per-
   sons in Dipper, 11
Sheridan, Wyo., Crow queen of
   rodeo, 134–35
Shoshoni Indians. *See* Sun
   Dance
Sioux Indians. *See* Dakota; Sun
   Dance
Star Persons, spirit beings, 15,
   23